MELUSI'S EVERYDAY ZULU

MELUSI TSHABALALA

Melusi's Everyday Zulu

There is um'Zulu in All of Us

Jonathan Ball Publishers
Johannesburg & Cape Town

Originally published in South Africa in 2018 by
JONATHAN BALL PUBLISHERS
A division of Media24 (Pty) Ltd
PO Box 33977
Jeppestown
2043

ISBN 9781868429066
ebook ISBN 9781868429073

Every effort has been made to trace the copyright holders and to obtain
their permission for the use of copyright material. The publishers apologise
for any errors or omissions and would be grateful to be notified of
any corrections that should be incorporated in future editions of this book.

Twitter: www.twitter.com/JonathanBallPub
Facebook: www.facebook.com/JonathanBallPublishers
Blog: http://jonathanball.bookslive.co.za/

Cover by Kholiwe Sinuma, Studio 214
Design and typesetting by Nazli Jacobs
Editing by Angela Voges
Proofreading by Thenjiwe Mswane and Paul Wise

Set in Dante

Printed by **novus print**, a Novus Holdings company

To my children:
Tumelo, Azande and Akhile,
you are my everyday inspiration.

Contents

Introduction

▼▲▼

You're probably thinking, '*Melusi's Everyday Zulu*? Heh, bantu. Who is this Melusi? Why should we care about his everyday Zulu? Why does he even get to have his own Zulu?'

These are all valid questions. I would have asked them too had I ever come across a similarly titled book by some random author. I'll try to answer as best as I can, and put you at ease about who I am and how this book came to be.

First things first: isiZulu has not been appropriated. I do not have my own isiZulu. IsiZulu used in this book will be familiar to isiZulu speakers. The only reason why this book is titled *Melusi's Everyday Zulu* is because I wrote it. Somebody else could have done the same thing, but they didn't. In addition, I use my take on the world and my experiences as a Zulu man who is navigating his way through twenty-first-century Africa to bring words esiZulu to life in a way that is entertaining and engaging.

Okay, now that's out of the way, let me tell you more about myself and how the book came about.

Born in Soweto on the 14th of December 1977, I have been um'Zulu all of my life.

If you're reading this in 2018 when the book was first published, 1977 is forty years ago. If you're reading this before 2018, you're a time traveller and I would love to learn your ways, chief. If you're reading this years after 2018, thank you for keeping the movement alive.

I was born um'Zulu in Baragwanath Hospital and have managed to remain um'Zulu since then. There is a brief, dark period where I almost became um'Tswana, but thankfully it didn't take hold.

Throughout my time as um'Zulu I have spoken isiZulu whenever I can. I say 'whenever I can' because South Africa has ten other official languages and sometimes you have to speak them. I have no problem with this because I respect and enjoy other languages. I prefer isiZulu, though. It comes more naturally to me. I think, when I was born, I cried in isiZulu.

That said, living in Johannesburg and working in corporate South Africa means one also speaks a lot of English. Too much, in fact. One also writes in English way more often than in one's mother tongue. If you are not careful, you could lose touch with your mother tongue. Many have.

The risk this poses to our mother tongues is one of the reasons I started posting an isiZulu word on my Facebook profile every day. Another reason is that I've worked in the advertising industry since 1998 and have been disgusted by the disregard with which the industry treats African languages. It matters greatly how advertising treats our languages because the industry spends gazillions of rands every month on creating and running radio ads in those languages. Yet we are bombarded with adverts that often hurt our feelings because of how they treat these languages.

I started posting one isiZulu word or expression a day on Facebook in October 2017. I did so on my personal Facebook profile, so only my friends saw the posts. We'd all have a laugh. Then, one day, I came out of a meeting to about forty new Facebook friend requests.

This was odd but not alarming, so I went to my next meeting. When I came out of that meeting, I checked my Facebook profile again. By then, I had about three hundred new friend requests. This was definitely alarming. Had my account been hacked? I'd usually get about ten new friend requests a day – what the hell was going on? Before that day was over, I had received about two thousand new friend requests.

Even more alarming, the requests were mostly from middle-aged white women. What did they want from me?

Then I remembered I had posted the word 'm'gabe', a township word that refers to the face you make when you want to show your displeasure or disapproval, or to intimidate someone. I'd explained that the word is derived from the surname Mugabe because when you make that face, you look as pissed off as Robert Mugabe.

Since it was posted during the week of the Zimbabwe coup, I figured the friend requests could be from former Rhodesians who thought I was pro-Rhodesia. Which I certainly am not. With hindsight, it makes no sense how I could even have arrived at that assumption.

Anyway, I contacted an older white friend (a former employer, who also features in one of the stories in the book), told him about the friend requests, and asked whether he thought they were Rhodesians. I figured that, since he was a middle-aged white person, he'd know how other middle-aged white people think.

I was right. He laughed and told me to stop being silly; the requests were probably from people who enjoyed the isiZulu posts and wanted to read more. That put me at ease a bit, but I was still sceptical; my past experiences with white people had left me jaded.

Sitting in traffic a little later, I decided, to hell with it. After all, what was the worst thing that could happen? *If these people turn out to be racist assholes, I can just unfriend them*, I thought.

So, I began to accept the requests. By this time, the number had risen to two thousand and something, and continued to rise. I managed to accept all that day's requests, and have accepted many more since. In fact, the following grew to a point where I had to set up a separate Melusi's Everyday Zulu Facebook page. I now post on my personal page and that page.

While running a page that is followed by people from all walks of life and from across the world is deeply satisfying, it is not without its challenges. I have been condemned by Christians for blasphemy. I've been called out for misogyny (rightly so) – and I apologised after taking a long, hard look in the mirror.

I have had to block racists. But, surprisingly, I've had to deal with far fewer racists than I thought I would. That has been one of this initiative's pleasant surprises. The other surprise is just how much people really want to learn about other people's cultures. While the page is definitely about isiZulu, the discussions go beyond that; we all learn so much about one another and the fascinating worlds in which we live, love and laugh.

I am no isiZulu expert. What I do is share what I know, and introduce the language in a fun way. *Melusi's Everyday Zulu* is not intended as a language course, but merely to pique your interest in isiZulu. The book is an anthology of some of the jokes and stories originally posted on Facebook, and others that have been written specifically for the book. Enjoy – and, hopefully, learn some words and phrases that will come in handy in your interactions with fellow South Africans.

MELUSI TSHABALALA

Ngibonga . . .

▼▲▼

NGIBONGA . . .[1]

My mother turned sixty while I was working on this book, which inspired me to write about this word. 'Ngibonga . . .' is an incomplete sentence that means 'I thank . . .' As in, I thank my mother.

Ngibonga that she is the best mother I could ever have asked for. That lady had me when she was twenty and it ruined whatever plans she had for herself. Abandoning everything she was busy with, she settled for a life as a domestic worker. This is what she has spent the past forty years doing. It put a roof over our heads, kept us fed and put us through school.

Thank you so much.

Ngibonga her church buddies for always being there for her, even when her children fail her. Unfortunately it does happen. Not so often these days, though.

Ngibonga that she's such an awesome grandma.

Ngibonga that she forgave me for getting myself expelled from the lovely private school she and her employers had managed to get me into. I'm such an ungrateful piece of shit.

Ngibonga uZuma for finally stepping down. We no longer

have white people rubbing him in our faces. Shoo.

Ngibonga that the DA will now also have to tell us about their policies, instead of screaming 'Zuma' the whole time. What do you stand for, guys? Why should we vote for you?

Ngibonga that Cyril is a billionaire, because that means he can count up to a billion and beyond. Actually, I lie: I know crooked millionaires who can't count for shit.

Ngibonga uHelen Zille for colonialism. It's been a blast. Yes, I am now crediting her with it. She defends it so much she may as well inherit it.

Ngibonga i-alcohol for nothing. And for everything. It's a love–hate relationship, especially on Mondays.

Ngibonga that I don't smoke. It seems really kak.

Ngibonga my kids for not being complete shits.

Ngibonga iKalawa Jazmee for all the good times. Oh, so many good times.

Ngibonga the guy who punched me so hard my eye was swollen shut for a week. It helped me see myself clearly. This was a few years back.

Ngibonga my wife for bailing me out of Sandton Police Station, Douglasdale Police Station and Randburg Police Station. This was before the eye-opening punch.

Ngibonga you for buying and reading this book.

Melusi's Everyday Politics

▼▲▼▲▼

There is a quote by the Greek statesman, orator and general Pericles that reads, 'Just because you don't take an interest in politics, it doesn't mean politics won't take an interest in you.'

Quite ominous, neh? Ominous and true.

We should all be interested in politics because it affects our lives. But also because politicians are hilarious. They don't mean to be, but they are. Okay, Julius means to be funny. He goes out of his way to get laughs. He also goes out of his way to strike fear into the hearts of his adversaries. Eish, that guy.

Anyway, I follow politics quite closely and I am not scared to share my views. That said, if my body is found in a ditch somewhere, it's because of some of the things I say in this section.

ISONO

Isono is sin. My most favourite thing in the world. Kidding. I don't sin. Ever.

Isono also expresses pity. We feel pity for everybody, even those who've wronged us. Isono, shem.

When Silili[1] won the ANC presidency, I found myself thinking, *Isono ngo Zuma. He's going to jail.* I also found myself thinking, *Isono ngo Silili, shem. They are going to give him such a hard time, trying to keep Zuma out of jail. Wooo.*

Then I felt bad for Nkosazana, like, *Isono, shem. She backed the wrong side.*

There's also Ace Magashule, who really should simply have stayed in the Free State. Isono, shem. Now he must answer to all of us and that uncle can't answer nothing for shit. Isono shem, because we want answers.

Isono ngo Mmusi Maimane. Shem, man. Askies.

When those EFF kids trashed H&M, I felt so bad for the traumatised workers. Isono, shem.

Where is Helen Zille? She told us she stopped washing when Cape Town still had water. Isono nga loya gogo (we must feel pity for that granny).

What they're doing to Patricia de Lille: isono.

What she did to the PAC: isono.

PAC. Isono.

Where are Mbhazima Shilowa and his red socks? Isono, shem. Does he even use the Gautrain, formerly known as the Shilowa Express? I bet he is boycotting it.

Terror is gonna burst a blood vessel. Isono.

Which homeland did Bantu lead? Was it Transkei or Ciskei? I forget. Isono.

Where is Kortbroek? Isono, 'yazi.

How much time does Malusi Gigaba spend in front of the mirror? Isono.

---

1   Cyril Ramaphosa. See 'Is'piliyoni', p. 84.

Lynne Brown, what did you get yourself into? Have you watched that TV series, *The Lockdown*? Isono.

Bathabile, R500 000 to get interviewed? Isono, shem.

Have you seen that video of those Afrikaner kids getting trained for the war with black people? Shem. Isono. My kids want to be scientists, chefs and race car drivers. Killing people is not part of the agenda.

Poor South Africa. Isono. Yoooh.

But you can't feel isono for Mangosuthu. No. There will be none of that. He will not allow it at all.

DLISA

Dlisa is versatile word that means many different things, depending on its context. It is derived from dla, which is to eat in isiZulu.

In most Nguni languages, dlisa can be used in many different contexts, with each context ensuring a slightly different meaning.

Apart from meaning 'eat', dla is also 'spend', as in 'The Guptas ate our money'. It also means to forfeit, as in 'Your thing was eaten'. It can refer to having sex, as in 'I ate her', or losing at something, as in 'Arsenal always gets eaten'.

As such, dlisa is to feed. It is to be generous, as in 'uZuma udlisa amaGupta.' It is to cause to lose, as in 'uSteve Khompela uyadlisa.' So, it can go on and on, depending on the context.

However, right now, I want to talk about dlisa in the context of feeding someone love muthi so they only have eyes for you. That muthi is called bheka mina ngedwa (only have eyes for me). I don't know if it works or not, but some people swear by it.

19

My dream would be if we could dlisa our politicians bheka mina ngedwa. Give them umuthi that will make them fall deeply and madly in love with South Africa and South Africans. Thakatha (bewitch) them so all their decisions are made from a place of deep love for this country and its people.

Sure, they could still all have their different approaches and policies and we would still vote for the ones that resonate with us the most. However, we would know they all come from a place of love and simply have different views on how to make us – their beloveds – happy. They would also love us equally, regardless of race, gender, sexual orientation, religion or creed. There would be no bias and decisions would be made with the interests of the greater collective in mind.

Imagine Kallie Kriel and Pieter Mulder being deeply and sincerely concerned about my well-being and the future of my children.

Or every South African knowing for a fact that Julius Malema loves them and only wants the best for them, too.

Just imagine.

PHAPHA

Phapha is a word and a concept I wholeheartedly believe should be included in the English language. I don't know how English speakers can get through life without it. However, I do suspect Afrikaans has an equivalent. Because Afrikaans.

Over the years, I have tried to find the English equivalent of phapha and have always failed. So many times, I've needed to tell someone uyapahapha in English but no English word can deliver the same feeling or impact.

The word 'presumptuous', while a correct literal translation, sounds too pompous. 'Forward' is too simple. 'Fuck you' is way too much and reduces you to a foul-mouthed idiot, even if sometimes that's all you're left with.

Phapha is a derivative of phaphalaza, which is to career. So, when you phapha, your brain, personality or temperament is like a car that's out of control, as if it is being 'driven' by a stupid, incompetent buffoon. You open your mouth, but words come out your ass.

In short, you don't know how to mind your own business. There is no self-awareness and you have no sense of the world around you.

Phapha is a trusted, versatile and effective word that is part of every isiZulu speaker's vocabulary. Ukuphapha (to phapha) manifests in infinite ways and often ends in tears. It is the default setting of toddlers, politicians and Steve Hofmeyr.

Mmusi Maimane, uyaphapha (you phapha).

Julius Malema, uyaphapha. But he's improved tremendously. Fikile Mbalula, uyaphapha.

Helen Zille, uyaphapha.

That EFF lady who always insists on speaking isiZulu in Parliament, uyaphapha. Of course, there's nothing wrong with speaking your home language anywhere in South Africa, but she's an attention-seeker.

However, ukuphapha can also change the world. Abantu abaphaphayo (people who phapha) are often the flies in the status quo ointment. I imagine Verwoerd often used to think to himself, *Daai fokken Nelson Mandela, hy phapha*.

South Africa has many of these kinds of phaphists or omas-'phapheni (people who phapha all the time). They are people who will not allow you to bully them into sitting in a corner, sucking their thumbs. They will not be silenced or intimidated.

Thuli Madonsela is such a phaphist.[II] Just ask the former president and the Guptas.

Cassper Nyovest is also a phaphist. He obviously doesn't have me in mind when he makes music, but I can respect his hustle.

Desmond Tutu has been such a phaphist for longer than I've been alive.

Pravin Gordhan is such a phaphist. If only more Zuma ministers could have had his conviction. Hopefully some of them are going to be facing a different kind of conviction, though.

Caster Semenya is another such a phaphist. Where does she get off taking on the world like that? We love it.

The millions of youngsters living in dire poverty while still chasing their dreams are also such phaphists.

Only history will tell us whether Malema is this type of phaphist, or a garden variety phaphist.

USATHANE

uSathane is Satan – the devil.

uSathane is not giving us a chance to come up for air. We are still busy dealing with the effects of apartheid, ongoing racism, rampant crime, white supremacy, sexism, homophobia, misogyny, patriarchy, poverty, xenophobia, gender and race-based wage gaps, e-tolls, white monopoly capital, guys with halitosis, a crap education system and drug and alcohol abuse. So, you'd think we have enough on our hands. But no: uSathane goes and adds state capture to the mix.

Hayi, man! Why couldn't they capture the state later and let us at least finish dealing with what's already on our plates? Give us a fighting chance?

uSathane also brought the people of the Western Cape and Eastern Cape crippling droughts, when they least needed them. Not that anyone ever needs a drought. But you know what I mean.

POPEYE

Spinach junkie and sailor man Popeye is known and loved the world over. He is the protector of dainty Olive Oyl, the adoptive father of Swee'Pea and the nemesis of Bluto.

The word 'popeye' has been an important part of black South Africans' lexicon for a very long time. It's used across the board (not just in isiZulu) as the word for cartoons, comics, animation and graphic novels. From Mickey Mouse, the Bafanas and Dennis the Menace to Superman, explainer videos and Madam & Eve – they are all amapopeye/opopeye. ('Ama-' and 'o-' are both plural prefixes. In this context, your choice of prefix will depend on regional and personal preference. I'm an amapopeye man. If you use the 'o', you will come across as more 'authentically' um'Zulu, though.)

Waking up to the news of 2017's junk status downgrade by S&P Global, many of us felt South Africa was officially a popeye nation with a popeye economy managed by popeye leaders who were acting at the behest of a popeye president.

There were amapopeye everywhere. It was unbelievable.

Thank goodness the other ratings agencies weren't as quick to downgrade us to junk.

Aside from the politicians, we all have amapopeye in our lives. Some people are married to them. Others work for or with them. Maybe you worship with one or play sport with one. But there is no environment that's not littered with amapopeye.

If you're in a room and you can't spot a popeye, then you should know – you're it.

When it's time to get serious, a great phrase to use is isikhathi samapopeye siphelile, which means the time for playing the fool is over.

Want your children to know you're no longer taking their shit? Iisikhathi samapopeye siphelile.

Want your boyfriend to know you're no longer bending over backwards? Isikhathi samapopeye siphelile.

Your friend wants to know why you don't drink any more? Isikhathi samapopeye siphelile.

BEKEZELA

Bekezela means have patience.

But it really has come to mean put up with nonsense. This word and concept have caused black people so much trouble. People stay in terrible jobs because of it. Our sisters stay in horrible relationships and marriages because of it. Some even end up dead because of ukubekezela. We put up with nonsense politicians because of ukubekezela. Bekezela also ruined lives through the Kaizer Chiefs–Steve Komphela shit show.

I suspect bekezela is what kept Madiba in prison for twenty-seven years. Me, I would have escaped. Twenty-seven years? Aneva!

From what I've seen, people who've freed themselves from this bekezela nonsense do much better in life. They are happier in the long term.

Except for Madiba, of course. His worked. Mara (but).

Bekezela goes hand in hand with another nonsense consideration – abantu bazothini (what will people say)? Pay attention to this and you will go nowhere and achieve nothing.

You can miss me with your bekezela as your boss browbeats you, day in and day out. You can bekezela on your own as your wife feeds you gluten-free swill. Go on, bekezela as your boyfriend runs the streets. Bekezela, as the life you want and deserve passes you by.

Or don't.

The next time someone tells you bekezela, respond with 'Bekezela yamasimba (Have patience se gat),' then karate chop them in the throat. Usually it's older black women (moms) who tell people to bekezela. Don't karate chop them. That's just not on. In fact, don't karate chop anyone in the throat, unless they are attacking you. If you're a black woman, stop telling younger people to bekezela, especially younger black women. They might karate chop *you* in the throat.

If our politicians don't pull finger, and soon, I suspect South Africa's new slogan will officially be bekezela as things continue to get worse and worse. Come on, say it with me: No more bekezela. Isikhathi samapopeye siphelile (the time for playing the fool, or putting up with fools, is over).

DUDUZA

Duduza means to comfort, and is the word on which the names Duduzane, Duduzile (Myeni), Mduduzi (Manana), Helen Dudu-Zille and baba ka Duduzane are based. Oh, the irony.

Anyway, enough about this bunch of non-comforters.

An uncle of mine once told me that the word duduza comes from the sound made when you hug someone and pat them on the back to comfort them. If that's the case, how hard were the ancestors patting each other on the back for them to make a 'du du' sound? Even if you use a bit of force, it just makes a slapping sound; to achieve a 'du du' sound, you have to use a fist and thump the person. I don't see how that would duduza me. It would just upset me and the other party would then need to be duduza-ed, after getting an earful of swear words.

Maybe the ancestors were not comforting one another. Maybe they would pull you close, give you a violent thump on the back to knock some sense into you, and tell you to harden the fuck up.

'What? A leopard ate your girlfriend? Come in for a hug, buddy. Du du – harden the fuck up! The leopard did you a favour. She was a cheetah. Hahahaha, get it? She was cheating on you and a leopard and a cheetah … aargh, never mind.'

'What? Your neighbour lilizelas[III] (ululates)[2] the whole night as she and her husband go at it and you can't get any sleep? Come in for a hug, granddaughter. Du du – stop being a sourpuss. Get your own lover to make you lilizela the whole night too. It doesn't have to be a man.'

---

2   See 'lilizela', p. 198.

'What? The settlers are making you feel inferior? Come in for a hug, son. Du du – grow a spine and stop buying into that bullshit. You're fucking amazing.'

Look, I don't know whether my uncle was telling the truth about the origins of duduza. I doubt he was. In fact, I don't even think he was my uncle.

What I do know is that we shouldn't wait to be duduza-ed, especially by politicians. We need to harden the fuck up and take matters into our own hands if we want to get anywhere.

NJE

Nje means 'just because' and 'definitely'.

It's a mischievous, deviant and spiteful little three-letter word. Nje can bring adults to tears, topple leaders and cripple countries. There is devastating power in nje. Let me explain with some examples.

DUDUZANE: Are you really going help me and the Guptas capture the state?

DADDYZANE: Nje.

DUDUZANE: Why would you betray the people of this beautiful country and the movement you dedicated your life to?

DADDYZANE: Nje . . .

DUDUZANE: Let's do it, baba. Let's do it.

DADDYZANE: Nje!

And the rest, as they say, is history.

Nje was probably also Daddyzane's undoing.

DADDYZANE: DD, your branches are going to support NDZ?

DD (Mabuza): Nje.

DADDYZANE: Sure sure?

DD: Nje.

(*A little later*) DADDYZANE: DD, why did your supporters
go with Silili?

DD, now DP (deputy president): Nje.

DADDYZANE: You're lying. You were always going to screw
me so Silili could make you deputy president of the republic.

DD, now DP: Nje.

Toddlers, even non-Zulu toddlers, are in a permanent nje
mood.

MOMMY 1: Sipho, why did you bite the dog?

SIPHO: Nje.

MOMMY 2: Cindy, did you just glue your sister to fridge?

CINDY: Nje, bitch.

MOMMY: Why did you call me a bitch?

CINDY: Nje.

Ya, vele (of course), white toddlers swear. They do. I've heard
them.

And finally:

FLOYD: What are we doing tonight, Juju?

JUJU: The same thing we do every night, Floyd.

FLOYD: What's that, Juju?

JUJU: Try and take over the land.

FLOYD: Nje.

BUZA IPASI NES'PESHELI

Ipasi nes'pesheli is the Zulufied version of 'pass and special', as in your South African pass book (dompas) and the special permit that allowed you to be in an area where black people were otherwise not allowed. This, of course, is apartheid stuff.

Buza is to ask. It is not pronounced like boozer, because the b is slightly different. The expression is used to indicate that someone is irritating you by asking endless and often prying questions, just like an apartheid cop who is looking for a reason to lock you up. It is used thus: 'Yini ungibuza ipasi nes'peheli (why are you asking me for my pass book and my special permit)?' Or: 'Ungibuza ipasi nes'pesheli ... (You're asking me for my pass book and my special permit ...)' Or: 'Ungangibuzi ipasi nes'pesheli. (You must not ask me for my pass book and my special permit.)'

Of course, the use of buza ipasi nes'pesheli is meant to make you feel like a terrible (black) person for acting like an apartheid cop. The idea is to get you to back down.

Elders often use this tactic when they are caught out by younger people. For example, you think you saw granddad holding hands with one of the magrizas (old ladies) from church, so you want to know what the hell was going on. If he hits you with, 'Ungibuza ipasi nes'pesheli, ntombazanyana (little girl),' you just know the old dog is up to no good.

Poor gogo. She's had to deal with fifty years of this shit.

I also suspect former Number 1 used this tactic quite a lot at ANC NEC meetings. It works because some of those minsinsila kaSathane (Satan's butt cracks) were clearly undercover apartheid cops, hence they can't help themselves and continue to serve interests that run counter to the needs of our people.

So, when former Number 1 accused them of acting like apartheid cops, they thought he knew something about their askari pasts. Oh, the devastating power of smallanyana skeletons.

Buza ipasi nes'pesheli is, of course, not the only expression derived from apartheid laws and acts of brutality. Take, for example, uzowukhomba umuzi onotshwala.[3] Taken literally, this expression means 'you will point out the home with the booze'. This refers to how, during raids, shebeens would hide their stock – but apartheid police would beat you until you pointed out where the booze was hidden or which house was the shebeen.

Back in the late 1980s, whenever my youngest aunt or oldest cousin did something wrong and would not admit it, my grandmother would use this expression and we would know that imvubu (the sjambok) was coming out and we were all getting a beating. I would get a quick one-two because I was years younger than everyone. I would have died if I'd got the same level of sjamboking as them. If one of you messes up, you all suffer. She would have made a great apartheid cop.

The good thing about imvubu is that it's flammable. Bye-bye, imvubu. But because that imvubu was cheap, she'd have a new one, ready to go, the next day. Sometimes, she had a few stashed away.

UVALO

Uvalo is fear.

When excerpts from Jacques Pauw's *The President's Keepers*

---

3   (Uzo-)(wu-)khomba = (you will) point out, (u)muzi = (the) home, (ono-)tshwala = (with the) booze

were first published and the frightening allegations against then-President Jacob Zuma were made public, we were astounded. Yoh! It was sobering stuff. And frightening.

Reading the *Sunday Times* that morning, we all felt uvalo. I found myself thinking, *What the hell is going on? Is the president really up to all this stuff? If the excerpt has upset me so, then the contents of the actual book will probably fill me with the highest level of uvalo.*

The concept of uvalo – or, rather, of not having uvalo – has always been a part of our culture. But it gained real infamy when it was used as part of the messaging in the ANC's 2016 local elections campaign.

You remember #asinavalo, right? It was dissected to death in the media and everyone came to learn that it means we have no fear, or we are fearless. What they didn't tell you is asinavalo can also mean we are shameless. You'd think with so many isiZulu speakers in positions of power in the party someone would have raised their hand and, perhaps, said, 'Aninyi? (you've gotta be shitting me).'

Maybe it was intentional – a cry for help. They wanted us to know what was happening in the organisation so we would come to their rescue. Instead, we mocked them. Shame on us. Look now.

Since then, so much more has come to light, but we still don't know what's really going on. It's all too much. I still have uvalo.

ISINA MUVA LIYABUKWA

Isina muva liyabukwa is an expression similar to the English 'he who laughs last' or 'save the best for last'. In the Nguni context, it refers to dancing: he who dances last receives all the attention (sina = to dance; muva = behind or last; liyabukwa relates to buka, which is to look at).

During the days leading up to his resignation, I imagined Zuma walking out of a meeting of the ANC NEC and saying, 'Isina muva liyabukwa.'

NEC MEMBER 1: What the hell does he mean by that?

NEC MEMBER 2: The expression means ...

NEC MEMBER 1: I know what the expression means. I mean, why the hell is he talking about dancing last? He danced first. And he's been dancing throughout his term as president. WTF? He doesn't get to dance last. No. We are dancing last. The recall is the last dance, demmit. It's the last fucking dance.

NEC MEMBER 2: Screw this guy. Let's take away his bheshu (loincloth), his hawu (shield), isagila (knobkerrie) and izingxabulela (sandals).

NEC MEMBER 1: What the hell will that do?

NEC MEMBER 2: It'll leave him without dancing regalia. Surely, he won't dance without his regalia.

NEC MEMBER 1: God, you're a fucking idiot. Which branch voted you into the NEC? I bet you're from some Buttfucksdorp in the Northern Cape.

NEC MEMBER 2: Hey, man. You're being a poes now. I'm not the enemy here.

NEC MEMBER 1: You're right. I'm sorry, comrade. What I meant is not having his dancing regalia won't stop him from dancing. The emperor has been walking around, buck naked, without a care in the world.

NEC MEMBER 2: Shit, you're right.

NEC MEMBER 1 (grossed out): We've seen his nutsack.

NEC MEMBER 2 (almost puking): He's been teabagging us, man.

NEC MEMBER 1: Isende lendlela.[4]

(They fall silent.)

NEC MEMBER 2 (excitedly): I know, I know – let's cancel the dance altogether.

NEC MEMBER 1: That won't help. He'll just dance alone and declare himself the winner.

NEC MEMBER 2: Isende lendlela.

IQANDA

Iqanda is 'egg' and 'zero'.

I remember seeing a newspaper headline with the hashtag #ZumaQandA and thinking, *What is this now? What has Zuma done to whose egg?* Then, the part of my brain that gets English and its concepts switched on, and I realised it was Zuma Q and A. Bloody hashtags.

This was at a time when newspapers carried story after story of the then president's endless troubles. When I saw that

---

4   Isende lendlela means 'the road ahead is still long'. Isende is shorthand for iseyinde, and is related to the word 'de', which means long/far/tall. Ndlela is 'way' or 'road'.

   Isende also means testicle, so by using this expression you also show your displeasure about the lengthy road ahead. Note: iseyinde/isende (long/far/tall) and isende (testicle) are not related.

   Let's say you're in a pointless brainstorming session and are visibly not happy so your boss asks, 'What's wrong, Lodewikus?'

   You can respond despondently, 'Isende lendlela.'

headline, I immediately felt for the man. Regardless of who a person is, when trouble follows them like that, you have to start feeling for them. Surely, at the height of the media on-slaught, he felt he was on a hiding to iqanda and that is a terrible feeling.

I know some people are reading this and wondering why I would sympathise with the man, because he brought it upon himself. It's only human to sympathise, guys. I'm only human. And the ex-president is also human. A human with a big, fat iqanda on his face. We've all been there. Maybe not at the same scale, but we've all had iqanda on our faces.

ULAMTHUTHU

The expression 'ulamthumthu – inkukhu yom'shini, enethwa ife' may seem complicated, but it simply means 'coddled weakling'. uLamthuthu is the key word here. uLamthuthu is also a type of chicken (a battery hen).

The rest of the words just give context. In case you don't know what a lamthuthu is, inkukhu yom'shini spells it out (literally, 'machine chicken'), while 'enethwa ife' means 'that dies the moment it gets rained on'. As a complete expression, it means a coddled weakling who, just like a battery hen, cannot handle the rains (of life).

You see, if you're going to keep free-range chickens, don't let a farmer trick you into buying battery hens, as they might roll over and die. They are just not used to the natural environment.

So, you can call someone ulamthuthu and be done with it. But for the full effect, you have to use the whole expression. Here's how the expression might be used:

ANC GAUTENG: Cyril, Cyril – he's our man. If he can't do it, no one can!

ANC KZN: Don't tell us about Silili Lamaphosa – that lamthuthu.

ANC GAUTENG: Did you just call CR17 inkukhu yom'shini?

ANC KZN: Enethwa ife.

ANC GAUTENG: How dare you?

ANC KZN: Yeah, we said it.

PS: I am not saying Silili is ulamthuthu. I just imagine that's what (some) people in the KZN ANC think. But he showed them, didn't he?

KHUMBULA

Khumbula means both 'miss' and 'remember'.

No, not miss as in, 'Excuse me, Miss, you're pretty and all but you need a breath mint.' Nor is it miss as in missing your ex-husband with your car as you drive away from divorce court. It's 'miss' as in missing Spoti because your ex-wife got him in the divorce. Spoti is a typical township dog name, along with Rex, Danger and Killer, and Spoti doesn't have to have spots.

It makes sense for the same word to be used for remember and miss. However, you can definitely remember people and things without missing them. For instance, I remember Miss Katzourakis (my Geography teacher) but I sure as hell don't miss her.

From early in 2018, the ANC and EFF played out a live version of *Khumbul' Ekhaya*, a show on SABC that helps people who are searching for missing family members. We were captivated. Would Julius return to the family he'd left under a dark cloud now that the uncle who used to touch him inappropriately had been excommunicated? Would he abandon his new ragtag family of urchins and an old-school *Ben 10* in favour of the big cookie jar he had access to while part of the ANC family? We stayed tuned so we wouldn't miss out on the unfolding drama.

Khumbuza is related to khumbula. Khumbuza is 'remind' or 'cause to miss'. When Cyril first reached out to Juju, did it khumbuza Juju of the good times at Luthuli House? There were some great times, all right. Or did it khumbuza Juju of Marikana? Perhaps it khumbuza-ed[IV] him that Cyril was the one tasked with kicking him out of the family …

As we remain enthralled by this story, it reminds us that there are no permanent friends or enemies in politics. Hearts get broken all the time.

Hey there, DA.

NDUNA and NSUMPA

Nduna is both a leader and a pimple. Nsumpa is both a wart and a principal.

Now, what do you think that says about our relationship with authority?

UNDUNANKULU

uNdunankulu means 'premier'. As in David Makhura is uNdunankulu of Gauteng.

Nduna is an isiZulu title, meaning chief, headman, commander, boss, foreman, or various other authority figures. It's also a term of endearment. Nkulu, on the other hand, means big. So, uNdunankula is essentially 'big boss'.

uNdunankulu is obviously not to be confused with ndun' enkulu (ndunu enkulu) which means 'big ass'. Nduna = chief; ndunu = ass.

Of course, there's nothing stopping someone with a big ass from becoming a premier. In that case, you'll then have uNdunankulu wendun' enkulu. We've seen this before.

There's also nothing stopping a premier from *being* a big ass. In this case, we have uNdunankulu oyindun' enkulu. This, we've also seen.

uNdunankulu is unisex, so Helen Zille is uNdunankulu of the Western Cape, while Nomvula Mokonyane is the former uNdunankulu of Gauteng. Interestingly, Nomvula once promised to defend former President Zuma with her ndun' enkulu. While Helen may not have indun' enkulu, many of the people in Western Cape townships and farms (and beyond) think she is one.

(Induna is also a pimple. So, a big pimple is induna enkulu.)

USOPOLITIKI

Usopolitiki means politician.

The prefix uso- in this instance means 'one who is involved with'. Oso- is the plural.

The reason why politicians are more concerned with politics than serving the people can be found in the construction of the word usopolitiki. We should start calling them political servants or helpers. That way, they don't go into a career in politics, but into a career of serving or helping the people.

In isiZulu, a politician would be um'sizi – helper. Um'sizi is related to siza – to help.

Umsizi is also 'pencil lead'.

Usizi is sorrow, which is what osopolitiki currently bring us.

Interestingly, when listening to or watching weather reports, I always feel usizi for isolated thundershowers. They must be so lonely. Then I remember that rain is not sentient, just like some politicians.

UM'HLALA PHANSI

Um'hlala phansi is retirement. There are two key words here: hlala (sit) and phansi (down). Isn't that awesome? Sit down and relax. Let the young people run around, making things happen. You've done your bit.

This is obviously not so great if you didn't plan properly for your retirement or were unable to because of the field of work you were in or simply because you were unemployed. This is the unfortunate case of so many South Africans. It is heartbreaking.

Then you have ANC politicians. Kanti[5] is there no um'hlala phansi age in politics? Besides land issues, the only other reason there could be to relook our Constitution is to include an um'hlala phansi age for politicians. Especially for those in the executive.

---

5   See 'Kanti', p. 181.

This is not ageism. Ageism is not having an um'hlala phansi age stipulated and enforced.

Come on, guys. You know a lot of our politicians need to hlala the fuck phansi and write memoirs. They all have amazing stories to tell and we would love to read them. We would take their life stories over their stale ideas any day. Tell us how you bombed the power station in 1960. Please. We just don't want your ideas about the Inter-whatchamacallit. Mkhulu and gogo, allow young men and women with new ideas to steer the ship. Please. Hlala phansi.

The world over, leaders are getting younger. At the time of writing this piece, France, Ireland and Estonia had elected people who were under forty, while Belgium, Greece, Malta and Luxembourg had gone for under-forty-five-year-olds.

Yet we are saddled with apartheid relics on all sides of the ANC spectrum. Now, before you point out that Mmusi is young, let me point you back to the word 'ideas'. Of course, there is also Malema, but he scares the other kids.

However, the ANC is probably still going to be in charge for some time. So, it is they who need to retire their elders and inject new blood into their organisation and the country. Looking at the ANCYL, we are in trouble, though. Those ones need to take early um'hlala phansi and piss off. Yes, sit down and futsek.

Say it with me, comrades: 'Um'hlala phansi! Ngowethu!'

Um'hlala phansi ngowethu is a play on 'Amandla! Ngawethu!', a well-known cry meaning 'the power is ours'.

IMPICA BADALA

When, on the morning after the Zimbabwe coup, we woke to a world where Robert Mugabe was still president of Zimbabwe, most South Africans and Zimbabweans were dumbfounded. It was a real impica badala (the 'c' in mpica is a click; it's not impikha).

Impica badala is a something that is so confounding that even the elders can't work it out. Impica is a riddle, while badala means 'of the elders'.

The thing to note here is the implied reverence for the wisdom of the elders. It's not impica ba-rich or impica ba-famous. Neither is it impica ba-sexy or impica bo-Google.

When all's said and done – when the tweets have been twittered, the grams insta-ed, the whats apped and the faces booked – true wisdom and the answers to life's most important questions lie with our elders.

Elders like Mugabe, Trump and Zuma. These are the people we should look up to for solutions about how to live in a new world. They have the vision, the ideas and the will to propel the world forwards and ensure that humanity performs at its best in the twenty-first century. By them, we are led.

NOT!

Seriously, WTF? I'm afraid to say, these days you can't take elders anywhere without them grabbing people by the cookie, getting their hands stuck in the cookie jar or being downright coupcoup (political analyst Ayesha Kajee's word).

Disclaimer: No elderly people were harmed in writing this explanation. If any elderly person is offended, I apologise. But if the offended elderly people (not the elderly people mentioned above) are serial lunatics, misogynists, liars, bigots and thieves, then I don't apologise. In fact, 'tsek.

ISIKHOKHO

If you've ever washed a pot in which pap or mielie rice (what's mielie rice? you ask) has been cooked, you've had to deal with isikhokho. Man, it's a pain.

Isikhokho is the hardened crust of pap or mielie rice that sticks to the bottom of the pot and simply won't come off. If you're using an old Hart-type pot with dents at the bottom, the job of removing isikhokho becomes even harder because bits of the crust get stuck in the nooks and crannies. You'll find yourself chiselling away with a spoon to the incessant rhythm of kho, kho, kho, kho while sweat runs down your face.

Dealing with isikhokho is no way to go through life. Obviously, some people have never had to wash their own pots, so they have no idea what I am talking about. But trust me, isikhokho is tough and unyielding. I've seen it bring grown women and men to the verge of tears.

So, the next time you see your maid looking teary-eyed, it's not because she's so grateful she has you as her wonderful employer. No, she's just been in an epic battle with isikhokho and most probably imagining it's you she's gouging with that spoon. Just kidding, your maid does not want to stab you to death with a kitchen utensil. (Or does she?)

Isikhokho is respected and feared in equal measure. That is how it became part of the everyday black South African lexicon outside the kitchen. You see, s'khokho, shorthand for isikhokho, is a term that also acknowledges an individual's awesomeness.

Our country is gifted in the s'khokho department. I would like to honour South Africa's biggest s'khokhos, people whose awesomeness cannot be messed with, just like the s'khokho stuck to the bottom of the pot. If we had S'khokho Awards to honour the amazing women, men and children of this land, my three nominees for the country's S'khokho of All Time would be:

My mother. She is is'khokho because she raised two boys and put them through school on her earnings as a domestic worker. Countless other parents also continue to beat seemingly insurmountable odds to build solid futures for their children; they are also izikhokho (plural). And no, my mother has never stabbed any of her employers with a spoon. She wouldn't hurt a fly, even though she used to be quick with the belt.

Nelson Mandela. We know why he's is'khokho.

The average South African. We are izikhokho (plural) because of our resilience, activism and undying spirit of optimism in the face of crippling poverty, unemployment, crime, corruption, violence, and the beast of structural racism. I salute you, zikhokho.

We are still hopeful that Mr Cyril Ramaphosa will be the s'khokho that helps get the ANC and, ultimately, the country, back on a path towards prosperity for all.

PS: Soaking the pot makes it easier to deal with isikhokho.

BOPHA

Bopha is to tie up, bind or arrest.

This makes perfect sense, because if you've been arrested, you're essentially tied up or bound.

To me, it makes sense that we should bopha everyone in the country. No, not only those in government. We should bopha everyone because it seems we're all up to shit. I don't trust any of us any more. We are all clearly a bunch of dodgy scumbags and national incarceration is the only solution.

Everyone will be guilty until proven innocent. Those who are out of the country must come back and non-South Africans must go home for a while to give us space to deal with this matter. Those who don't want to go all the way home can hang out in neighbouring countries until we're done. I hear Namibia is very spacious and the Windhoek Lager is free there.

When all foreign-based South Africans have returned home, and our guests from other countries have excused us, we should lock the gates and will all officially be under arrest. Then, the trials can begin. There will be individual and group trials.

The individual trials are for ordinary South Africans and group trials are for politicians, business leaders, church leaders, schoolteachers, bankers, cops, etc.

The charge is treason. For everybody.

Yes, we bopha everybody for treason because it seems we're collectively betraying this wonderful place. Treasonous acts are being committed from all quarters of our society.

If you think you're innocent, don't worry, you'll have your day in court. And I am pretty sure you'll be found guilty and you know why. Don't pretend you don't. I definitely know why I'm going down. Oh, I know.

To lead this process, we need someone who champions justice, is impartial and has a low tolerance for treason. To this end, I deem Kim Jong-un best for the positions of lead investigator, prosecutor and judge.

It's time for tough love, people. Isikhathi samapopeye siphelile (the time for playing the fool is over).

Melusi's
Everyday Reminiscences

▼▲▼

I turned forty while writing this book. This milestone was a big deal for me. A big, depressing deal.

Even though I knew it would happen, because everyone ages, I was in denial. I'd somehow convinced myself that I'd remain a vibrant youth forever. I should have joined the ANC Youth League: no one ages in that organisation. Well, I didn't join them, and I turned forty.

Hitting the big four-oh inspired me to look back on my life. In this section I touch on some of those memories.

AMA-

Ama- is a plural prefix. It's not the only isiZulu plural prefix, but it's the one best known by non-Zulu speakers.

In the late 1990s, I was a junior creative at advertising agency Leo Burnett. It was the best of times, it was the worst of times. Making the worst of times even worse was one member of the management team who used to treat black creatives like scum every chance she got. I forget her name, but vividly remember how much we all hated her.

This one time, I found our chance for revenge. She'd sent out a mail to the whole agency, asking, 'What is ama, as in amabhokobhoko, amagluglug and amakrokokroko?'

In my infinite wisdom, I figured that, if I deleted my e-mail address on my end, my response would be sent anonymously. I did just that and responded to the whole agency with, 'When a stupid person asks a lot of stupid questions, you say AMA-MORON!'

A few seconds later, I heard laughter ring around the agency and knew I'd hit the spot. Then a mail came in from the MD, summoning me to his office about the response I'd just sent.

My heart almost stopped. Because at that agency black creatives lived in constant fear of losing their jobs, I didn't go straight to the MD's office; I called my mother to tell her I'd lost my job. Then I walked to various offices to say my good-byes to the homies. That's when I learnt ukuthi (that) there is no such thing as sending mails anonymously. I was done for, man. Finished.

Eventually, I mustered the courage to walk into the MD's office. As soon as I walked in, he got up and walked past me to close the door. Then, instead of shouting at me or handing me a letter informing me of the termination of my employment, he covered his mouth with his hand and started laughing into it. For a really long time. I was so confused.

When he finally managed to catch his breath, he spoke: 'Man, you're brave. You know she's a board member, right? You've got some balls.'

Me (hesitant): 'In my defence, I thought ...'

MD: 'It's okay, man. Everybody hates her. I'm just gonna pretend I've reprimanded you and you are going to walk out of here, looking really sad, and go say you're sorry to Ama-Moron.'

As I was walked out, I could hear him laughing again.

MELUSI

Melusi is my name. It's also the isiZulu word for Jesus. Just kidding. It's his nickname. You see, Melusi means 'shepherd' and Jesus is your shepherd. So there.

Then there is Malusi, as in Malusi Gigaba. Melusi is spelled with an 'e', while Malusi has an 'a'. Melusi is pronounced Meh-loosy, while the other is Mah-loosy. They mean exactly the same thing – the difference in spelling is regional. Both names also feature in other languages.

Did Zulu parents name their children Melusi before the introduction of Christianity and Jesus the shepherd? I don't see why not. I'd hate to think my name is a product of coloni-alism.

Speaking of Melusi and Christianity, let me share a story.

My mother used to drag me to church – until one fateful day when I was sixteen years old. She had, once again, dragged me to a church in Chiawelo, Soweto, a dual-language Assemblies of God church.

The service is in isiZulu and Xitsonga. The preacher calls visitors to the front so they can introduce themselves; my mother forces me to go. I go last. The preacher says I should introduce myself. I oblige.

ME: Igama lami nguMelusi. (My name is Melusi.)

TSONGA TRANSLATOR: Libito lamina yiMorris. (My name is Morris.)

WTF?

ME: Baba, angiyena uMorris. NginguMelusi. (Sir, I am not Morris. I am Melusi.)

TRANSLATOR: AniMorris niMorris. (I am not Morris. I am Morris.)

ME: Baba, angisiwuMorris. NginguMelusi. (Sir, I am not Morris. I am Melusi.)

TRANSLATOR: AniMorris niMorris. (I am not Morris. I am Morris.)

As I am about to complain again, the preacher tugs at my shirt.

PREACHER: Akathi uwuMorris. UMelusi ngesiShangane wuMorisi. (He is not saying you are Morris. In Xitsonga, Melusi is Morisi.)

ME: Ohhhh, manje why etranslator igama lami? (Oh, but why is he translating my name?)

At that point, my mother indicates that I must meet her outside. Once outside, she says I never have to return to church if I don't want to. She says I am embarrassing her.

I've been to church many times since. But no one has called me Morisi again.

ISISHWAPHA

Isishwapha is a flat butt or no butt.

The size and shape of one's butt is an important thing, okay? There are, obviously, varying preferences, but everyone agrees isishwapha is no good, especially on women. Once again, as men we don't get judged by the same standards; women have it tough when it comes to butt politics.

As a kid, I once heard my mom and one of her sisters discussing the meanness of her sister's employer. They then laughed at the employer's isishwapha. Man, did they laugh. I had never heard them laugh so heartily. It emboldened me to butt in (childish pun obviously intended) and ask a question: 'Ma, why do white people have izishwapha (plural of isishwapha)?'

For once, she didn't slap me for butting into a grown-up conversation. Instead, she answered me enthusiastically: 'White people sit around and do nothing the whole day, while we do all the hard work. They sit in their offices, in their cars and in front of their TVs, so their butts don't grow.'

This explanation made sense to me, but I had another question, 'But Aunty Whatwhat sits around and does nothing all day and she still has a huge butt.'

That's when the slap came. Her hand flew through the air and landed on my cheek making a 'shwaaaaa phaaa' sound. That's when I figured God probably spanks mean people on their butts and that's how they end up with isishwapha. Of course, it would later turn out that this was also not the case and that my mom's explanation was a lie.

Some people have isishwapha, while others have asses. And that's that.

However, Afrikaans girls' asses seem to be getting bigger and bigger as apartheid fades further and further away. Hahahaha.

ITHANGA

Ithanga means both pumpkin and thigh.

Oh, thanga, thanga, thanga. Oh, how we love thee. Wars have been fought over ithanga, empires destroyed, families torn apart; friend has killed friend over ithanga.

I've got to tell you, I love me some good pumpkin. I mean,

who doesn't? Even as a young boy, I knew I was an ithanga man. Other boys at school would talk about melons and other fruit and veggies, as boys do, but I was only interested in ithanga.

Even at home, they knew. Every time my mother would say, 'Melusi, hamba uyothenga ithanga (Melusi, go buy pumpkin),' I'd get so excited. She never understood why. Just hearing the word ithanga would send me into a tizz. It still does.

Sunday meals were always my favourite – so much ithanga. I could have all the thanga I wanted. Others would have the proverbial seven colours, but on my plate there'd be only chicken thigh and ithanga. Give me thigh and ithanga any day and I am a happy man.

In my early twenties, I tried my hand at amathanga (plural) collecting. I tried my best to get my hands on one ithanga after the other. Amathanga, amathanga, amathanga. Ya, neh. It got me into a lot of trouble and hurt some wonderful young women. I am sorry.

BUMBA

Bumba is the act of moulding, shaping and creating. You can bumba a relationship, a nation, a child and even a business.

On the other hand, ubumba is clay, which can be moulded to create all manner of stuff, from toys to crockery. Growing up, in church we were told that God moulded man from ubumba (clay) then breathed life into that clay and it became Adam.

Because we were kids, this made perfect sense and inspired us to spend hours at the river, using ubumba to mould the things we wished for in the hope that they would somehow become real. We moulded cars, planes, clothes, the delicious food we saw in magazines. Some kids even moulded dads. None of these things materialised, except maybe the dads, but they were mostly temporary; just like the planes and cars we had moulded, when left unattended, the dads cracked and eventually crumbled.

Then we got to high school, and they told us that people and animals are made of chemicals. WTF? What about ubumba? What about Adam? What about Eve, who had been made from his rib?

When we got back home, we wanted answers, but no clear ones were forthcoming. This strained relations with the elders.

But clay bore the brunt of the anger. We all agreed: to hell with ubumba. It was not magical. We now saw it for the useless mud it really was. We even discouraged the younger kids from playing with it and shared our new knowledge with them. We became proper anti-ubumba activists and sparked a real ubumba uprising.

Today, when I see my younger kids playing with play dough and deriving so much pleasure from it, I am reminded of those ubumba days. Oh, what good times they were. I am not angry any more. I realise it allowed us to express our creativity and dream.

Until high school ruined everything. Damn you, high school, with your stupid science and facts. Sies.

I wish I could use ubumba again to make my dreams come true. I would bumba lots of money – billions, like Duduzane did. Then I'd retire to Dubai.

UBUGEBENGU

Ubugebengu is crime or criminal activity. It is related to the common word sgebengu or s'gebengu.

Speaking of ubugebengu, were the makers of Mainstay ever called to testify at the TRC? They should have been. I mean, to tell people living through apartheid that 'You can stay as you are for the rest of your life, or you can change to Mainstay' to an advertising tune so catchy is shooting fish in a barrel. It's criminal. Ubugebengu.

Even as a little kid, I remember thinking, *Hell no, I don't want to stay as I am, especially not for the rest of my life. I wanna change to Mainstay. And smoke some of that awesome Peter Stuyvesant, too. That's the life. Not this shit we're currently living through.*

Good thing Mom kept a very watchful eye over me.

PHAMBANA

Phambana is to mix up, cross paths, go against, intersect, or lose your mind (when the wires in your brain cross).

The related word uphambene is 'you're nuts' or 'he or she is nuts', depending on the intonation with the 'u' prefix, while the word for the Christian cross is isiphambano.

I grew up ezayoni, the Zionist church. In ezayoni, you have to wear a uniform and carry isiphambano (a staff in the shape of a cross). I didn't like church and my older cousin (may he rest in peace) liked it even less. We mostly disliked it because it went on and on. You'd be in church the whole day, while your friends, whose families were godless heathens or born-again Christians, were out on the streets, living their best lives. My mother would eventually become a born-again Christian, but my first experience of church was ezayoni.

My cousin would always say, 'Do you know why isiphambano is so important to churchgoers? Baphambene (they're crazy). Isiphambano is the universal symbol for ukuphambana. Hahahaha! Only people abaphambene would spend hours praying to an invisible man in the sky.'

Then I'd ask incredulously: 'Your mother uphambene?'

'Her uniform has isiphambano. Uphambene,' he'd respond.

'My mother?'

'Uphambene.'

'Ugogo?'

'Uphambene. Bonke (all of them) baphambene.'

He'd then proceed to prick those churchgoers who'd been taken over by the Holy Spirit with a needle to prove they were faking. And sure enough, they'd feel the pricks and squeal in pain. He figured that, if you were truly under the influence of the Holy Spirit, you wouldn't feel pain, otherwise uphambene, pretending to speak in tongues.

My cousin was crazy – 100% phambene. Like most South Africans, and our politicians. Niphambene (you are all crazy).

ISICABUCABU

Isicabucabu is a spider.

So, in isiZulu, Spider-Man will be called iSicabucabu Man, Indoda eyisicabucabu (a man that is a spider) or Isicabucabu sendoda (a spider of a man). Ndoda is man. Well, all these names just sound like Irritating Man because isicabucabu sounds a bit like casula, which is the isiZulu word for irritate and spiders are generally viewed as nuisances.

I know there are women who are reading this thinking, *Yes, yes, you are all iSicabucabu Man.* I am so sorry we're like this; we should strive to do better. We really should.

But back to Spider-Man. In the 1980s, we had simulcast television shows and *Spider-Man* was dubbed into Setswana. I honestly think they never gave us an um'Zulu *Spider-Man* simply because iSicabucabu Man/Indoda eyisicabucabu/Isicabucabu sendoda would have ruined the legendary theme song. Seriously, try singing the *Spider-Man* theme song chorus using one of these translations. It's bloody ridiculous.

Just like Spider-Man.

Why hasn't there ever been a villain who simply whacked him with a big slipper? Splat, and no more Spider-Man. He is the wimpiest superhero.

Anyway. Due to the TV show being in a black language, Spider-Man was the most popular superhero in the country. He had all of us wishing we could shoot webs out of our wrists. Spidey was our adopted black superhero.

That 1980s *Spider-Man* is why I was so excited about the movie *Black Panther*. Finally, I could knock that isicabucabu off his perch on my superhero list. He is still number 2, though. Note, not English-speaking Spider-Man. English-speaking Spider-Man can make like isicabucabu and suck it.

Interestingly, a group called Slug of War did a rock version of the SABC *Spider-Man* theme song. It's a hot mess, like the insides of an insect that's been bitten by isicabucabu. They just winged it and didn't use an actual South African language. Clearly, they couldn't have been bothered.

Their version of the song was also eye-opening. It left me with the horrifying realisation that we sound alien to our fellow citizens. I'd always understood that English and Afrikaans speakers don't understand us, but I'd never thought about what they actually hear when we speak. They just hear gibberish. Ya neh. Isende lendlela.

FAKAZA

Fakaza is to chip in with your two cents' worth.

The story of my life is being woken at least once a week by the three amigos (my kids) with some ridiculous story that someone had finished the cornflakes in just three days. The two youngest ones always blame the teenager. Actually, they gang up on him, with the girl leading the charge as the younger brother fakazas.

To fakaza is often not appreciated – my eldest certainly doesn't appreciate it, greeting it with, 'Ufakazani, wena? (Why are you chiming in?)' If looks could kill …

Fakaza is also to speak as a witness. A witness is ufakazi. Ufakazi uyafakaza, even though the accused obviously doesn't appreciate the witness's two cents' worth.

In church ukufakaza means to bear witness to God's glory and share your story with the congregation. As a teenager, this was my favourite thing about church. You'd have these hot older girls and young women fakaza-ing[v] (obviously under duress from their mothers) about all the nasty things they used to get up to before the Lord saved them.

As a young boy, I would sit there thinking, *Oh, God! That sounds amazing. Why aren't there girls like you in my life? Why am I such a loser? I love you. Please do those things with me.*

You'd also get the older boys, young men and husbands, forced to fakaza about the rubbishes they used to be before the Lord showed them the light. They were my heroes, legends a growing boy could look up to. I especially liked the ones who were obviously shitfaced as they were fakaza-ing about the Lord's glory. You'd see that some of them were on the verge of tipping over, the fumes of the previous day's spirits mixing nicely with the Holy Spirit to get the whole place feeling a bit giddy.

The male rubbishes and the young free spirits were usually familiar with one another; you'd see them talking after the service, the mothers and wives shooting them looks of disgust.

-LISA

No, not Lisa, as in the name. In isiZulu, -lisa relates to the male gender. Umlisa and owesilisa mean a male person.

I did come across an um'Zulu Lisa once, but her 'Lisa' was short for Lisana ('it's still raining'). I doubt Lisana is a real isiZulu name. Her parents are probably the kind who want to give their children white names, but pretend they don't.

No, my mother didn't name me Melusi so she could call me Mel. Sathane.

Back to the name Lisa. At one of my first jobs – I think I was seventeen – I worked with a horrible woman called Lisa. I forget her surname, but she was Maria Lisa Something-something. Man, this lady was mean. She talked down to everyone. When you saw her walking towards you, you turned and walked the other way.

I don't remember whose idea it was, but she ended up being called mLisa. This was on account of her freakishly big right hand. Her left hand was fine, but the right hand was really big. It was like a frying pan with five mielie cobs attached to it. It made her look like umlisa. She definitely wasn't disabled. In fact, we would not even have noticed her hand had she not been such a horrible person.

Calling her mLisa made working with her bearable. Her

perpetual bad mood no longer bothered us. She'd say some horrible shit; you'd smile and respond, 'Okay, mLisa.' We had defeated the witch using isiZulu.

It was all going well until impimpi – a thoroughbred German Shepherd polisiehond that barks in Afrikaans – told on us. mLisa was not happy. Not at all. But it didn't matter, because the school holidays were over and we no longer needed the job.

Impimpi is a snitch.

THUMA

Thuma means send. As in Bra Hugh and Cyril's thuma mina (send me).

While thuma mina is a great declaration of your commitment to playing your part in building a better South Africa, it's a teenager's nightmare. Parents will thuma you until you want to cry. It used to happen to me; now I'm doing it to my kids, especially the teenage boy. I wait for him to get deep into his video game/book/TV show/movie, then I send him on some nonsense errand. You can see the murder in his eyes.

It's the circle of life, li'l man.

Your mother will get off a taxi close to the shops, walk home then send you to the shops. 'Whaaaaaat? You walked past the shops. You saw them. You know they're there. They've been there for years. What witchcraft is this? Ubuthakathi!'[6]

You obviously wouldn't say this to her, because she'd thuma a hot klap in your direction.

---

6   See 'Thakatha', p. 71.

Speaking of mothers who thuma hot klaps at their kids, I am still blown away by how mouthy some white children are. Shooo.

Anyway, Cyril Ramaphosa thuma-ed me to write this book. He just doesn't know he did. Someone, tell him.

PHOXEKA

Phoxeka is to be disappointed.

In my teens, I fell in love with Latino culture – the movies, the music, the rides. I loved all aspects of it. So, I was blown away when I spotted two cool Latino cats having a chat on a Jozi street. I had never seen Latinos in real life. I went for it, using a line from a movie I fell in love with as a teenager and still watch today: 'Vatos locos, carnale!'

The dudes turned around and one responded, 'Jou poes!'

Tjo, I guess they weren't Latino. Wow. Can you say phoxeka?

DALA

Dala is to create, to cause or to be old. Umdali is a creator and also refers to God, the creator. Mdala (mudala) means he or she is old.

Mark Zuckerberg created Facebook, so he is its umdali – creator, god. An adult is umuntu omdala. Umuntu is person. When you first try to assert yourself as a young person by saying you are umdala (grown up), grown-ups will often ask you, 'Udale bani? (Who did you create?)'

Any object that is old is indala. However, when a coloured youngster says 'dala or sala', he means 'do something or be left (sala) on the ground'. The first time I heard this expression, I was as a learner in Bosmont, Johannesburg. We were walking to the shops during break when three older teenage boys appeared and told us to hand over our cash.

When we said no, one of them said, 'Hey, Zulu! Do you wanna dala, Zulu laaitie?'

We were confused. Why was this gazi[7] calling us Zulu? What was this dala he was speaking of? What did he want us to create? We decided to walk on, but then another one of the gazis screamed: 'Dala or sala! Dala or sala!'

Even though we had no idea what he was saying, he was rabid, so we ran for our lives.

Once back at school, we were told what dala or sala means. We also worked out that, because Zulus featured so prominently in the political violence of the time, these young men were challenging us from the misguided notion that brawling with Zulus would increase their street cred.

We were right to run: we were in no position to dala anything and we sure as hell were no Zulu warriors, which meant we probably would have sala-ed[VI] on the ground. This would not have been ideal, because we had double-period Geography after break and Miss Katzourakis would have been pissed off had we not made it to class – even if we were bleeding to death on the street.

'Dala what you must' is another coloured expression and challenge to action. Run!

---

7   'Gazi' is a term of endearment used predominantly in the coloured community to mean blood, family, or friend. It is used by non-coloureds to refer to coloureds.

UFUNANI?

Ufunani means 'what do you want?' or 'what are you looking for?'

Have you noticed how some strangers greet you with such enthusiasm you can't help but be suspicious: 'What? Ufunani?'

A person will just walk up to you, smile broadly and greet you enthusiastically. You end up looking around to see if you're on some candid camera show and Leon Schuster is about to jump out and pull your pants down. You don't have undies on that day and haven't applied lotion, so even your big boy is ashy. The last thing you need is bloody Leon Schuster, pulling your pants down and exposing you in front of a whole shopping centre. So, you ball up your fists and ask, 'Yini (What)? Ufunani (What do you want)?'

That Leon Schuster is why black people are so wary of white people who smile at us for no reason. We subconsciously suspect they're part of Leon's cast and are angling for a gap to humiliate us. Not today, sathane. Not today.

XAKA

Xaka means both to confuse and to put someone in a bind.

The year was 1999 and we were at Sun City for the Loeries, which are advertising industry awards. Stumbling around drunk in search of a party, I bumped into a guy I knew, Sandile. He told me to come with him because he knew of a raging party in one of the hotel rooms.

I followed, but when we got to the room, there was no party. There was just one nervous young woman. I was confused. Before I could ask what the hell was going on, Sandile quickly excused himself, mumbling something about booze, and disappeared out the door.

The woman then told me there was no party and that she was the one who'd asked Sandile to get me to the room, because she really wanted to talk to me. She proceeded to tell me how much she liked me and thought we could spend time together and get to know each other.

WTF? She probably just wants to steal my kidneys, I thought.

My tequila-soaked brain burped out a response: 'It's really nice that you like me, sisi, but I'm gay.' I thought that would get her off my back and allow me to dash out and continue my search for a party. I was wrong.

The next moment she broke down, tears streaming down her cheeks. Hayi, man!

It turns out she wasn't crying because the great love of her life was into penis. Far from it. She said she was crying because she was so overwhelmed by my openness about my sexuality. It turns out she was actually lesbian and had been pretending to like men because she couldn't get herself to disclose her real sexuality. Ini (what)?

Still in tears, she asked me how I found the strength to be so open about my sexuality. Jesu!

Her tears were so genuine and her question so sincere that I couldn't just run, even though that's exactly what I should have done. So, I spent a good portion of my night counselling this woman on how to come out to her family, even though I knew nothing about doing something like this. We both eventually passed out in her room. The next morning, guys were telling me about their awesome adventures with straight party girls. Oho (a dismissive sigh).

To this day, the events of that night xaka me.

INHLAMBA

Inhlamba is a swear word.

I was part of a creative team working on a TV brief for some Long Tom Coca-Cola can. Our creative director at the time had hated everything we had presented to him. We were really frustrated.

While continuing to conceptualise, we came up with a non-sense idea where the viewer sees a young dude in front of his computer, holding a regular Coke can. As he stares at his computer, suggestively licking his lips and moaning, he starts stroking the can and it grows, eventually becoming the Long Tom can.

We laughed and laughed, like the twenty-year-old boys we were. Then it was back to serious work.

Another review came, and our creative director still hated everything. I think I remember him saying our TV scripts would only be mildly amusing if they gave us paper cuts and we bled to death. Yup, they were harsh times.

It was at this point that I saw my creative partner decide to throw caution to the wind and present the nonsense boner idea. I wanted to stop him. I wanted to run. I wanted to hide. I wanted to die. But I just sat there.

As he went through the story, I could see the creative direc-tor get redder and redder. My creative partner obviously wasn't seeing what I was seeing, because he just continued. As soon as my creative partner was done, the creative director screamed, 'WHAT THE FUCK IS WRONG WITH YOU TWO?'

I wanted to explain that I had not agreed to present this thing, but I was scared of my creative partner because he had muscles.

The creative director continued, 'THE NEXT TIME EITHER OF YOU COMES INTO MY OFFICE ASKING FOR A RAISE, I'LL TELL YOU TO GO STROKE YOUR PAYSLIP AND SEE IF YOUR SALARY GROWS. GODDAMNIT! GET THE FUCK OUT OF MY OFFICE!'

I think I was in tears at this point. The idea of never getting a raise again was just too much.

As we walked out of the creative director's office, my creative partner smiled broadly, obviously satisfied with himself. The bastard.

I swore at him with inhlamba that cannot be repeated and which made me feel much better about the whole thing. In the absence of being able to retaliate to my boss, using inhlamba on my creative partner was therapeutic. It was the first time I came to understand the cathartic power of inhlamba. Inhlamba is now a good friend of mine, but is also why my mother is not allowed near this book.

UKUGANGA

Ukuganga is 'to be mischievous'. The root word is ganga.

One night, a few years ago when I was still a creative director at a major advertising agency, I went out for a solid drinking session with my executive creative director, who also happened to be my friend. He then remembered that he had a bunch of production house showreels he needed to look at for a job I was not even part of. He went to his car, brought back the discs and told me to check them out over the weekend and give him feedback on Monday.

WTF? This had nothing to do with me. But he insisted I do it. Nx.[8]

In a huff, I grabbed the discs and left.

Anyway, I had not driven two kilometres when the cops pulled me over. Great. We'd been drinking for a few hours and I had no interest in spending the weekend in a jail cell getting penetrated. In fact, I have no interest in getting penetrated anywhere, ever. So, the prospect of getting arrested was terrifying.

The cops seemed to sense my fear because they did not even pretend to want to arrest me. They went straight to pointing out that I smelled like a brewery, and should give them 'cooldrink' and go to sleep.

I didn't have money on me. But you know what I did have? Bloody showreels. Lots of them. And I put them to good use.

ME: Eh, grootman, I don't have money. But I have something better.

COP 1: Ini?

ME: Can't get, can't tholokala[9] movies. They are not yet in cinemas, but I have them.

COP 2: For sure?

ME: Nje. Let me get them from the boot.

I got out the car, walked to the boot, opened it, and bam! A *Pulp Fiction* briefcase-type glow temporarily blinded the cops. When they regained their vision, they saw mountains of DVDs

---

8   Used to express annoyance, anger or disappointment.

9   Meaning that something is rare or not readily available.

with titles like *Fresheye*, *Velocity*, *Velocity Africa*, *Egg* and *Bouffant* written on them.

COP 2: Tjo, tjo, tjo.

ME: What did I tell you? What did I tell you? Who's the man?

COP 1 and COP 2: You're the man.

ME: I said, who's the man?

COP 1 and COP 2: You're the man!

ME: Hola.

We were high-fiving one another at this point.

ME: Okay. So, *Fresheye* is a horror movie about this successful doctor who loses his eyesight but gets an eye transplant. The problem is, he got the eyes of a crazy serial killer and he begins to see all the things the killer has seen and done. But, instead of reporting the crimes, he starts seeing things the killer's way and becomes a serial killer himself.

COP 1: Shiiiiiiit.

ME: Imagine working a case like that.

COP 2: Yoh, yoh, yoh. Never. It's witchcraft.

ME: White-people witchcraft.

COP 1: What's *Velocity*?

ME: Haaa, *Velocity*! Yeses. Do you remember the movie *Speed*?

COP 2: Sure.

ME: In the first one, they were on a bus. Then, in the second one, on a boat. Now, they are in a spaceship.

COP 1: What?

ME: Yeah. That's why this one is not called *Speed*, but *Velocity*. In space you don't deal will speeds, baba. It's velocity all the way.

COP 2: *Velocity Africa* yona?

ME: Same thing as *Velocity*, but the black guy doesn't die first in this one.

COP 1 and COP 2: Sure, sure.

ME: *Egg* is a lesbian romantic comedy about these two women who have their eggs frozen and are thrown into each other's lives when the facility where their eggs are stored is robbed. There is confusion about which eggs are whose. In the ensuing madness the ladies fall in love.

COP 2: Hayi, hayi.

ME: What? You're against lesbians?

COP 2: No, no, bhoza. I just don't like romantic comedies. (Bhoza is a colloquial word for boss, but is used to mean friend in this instance.)

ME: Hoh. I bet you'll love *Bouffant*. Lots of nudity.

COP 1 and COP 2: Hola, bhoza! Hola.

They took the discs and I went home. I still wonder what happened when they settled in to watch their awesome movies and only found adverts. Eish.

That was ukuganga on my part.

PS: Drinking and driving is not cool. It's not ukuganga. It's dangerous and selfish. You could ruin other people's lives – never mind yours. I was young and reckless.

ASIPHINDELENI

Asiphindeleni means 'let us go back'.

It's related to phinda (repeat) and phindela (go back). Whereas phindela can be taken as an instruction or encouragement to return, asiphindeleni is an invitation, asking that we return together.

Every so often at work, I find myself thinking asiphindeleni to the beach. Back to the crashing waves and sand between our toes. Asiphindeleni.

But then, why stop at returning to the beach? Why not asiphindeleni all the way to 2010 when Soccer World Cup fever was in the air and we were getting along better than we had in a really long time? The World Cup was like one long Christmas. Asiphindeleni.

Asiphindeleni to R5,85 to the dollar. That was in 2005. Please, asiphindeleni.

Remember when petrol (95) was R6,54 a litre and we thought that was high? It was in 2007. Asiphindeleni.

Oh, what a day when Bafana Bafana were crowned Africa Cup of Nations champions. Asiphindeleni to that Bafana Bafana, but give them this current crop's money.

Asiphindeleni to the twalatsa, because, unlike vosho,[10] it wasn't reserved for people with medical aid.

I remember when *Tsotsi* won the Oscar for best foreign language film. Asiphindeleni to that moment.

Asiphindeleni to real kwaito – 'Strawberry Goom Goom', 'Rea Di Busa', 'Is Fokol Is Niks', Thula Mabota, 'Dlala Mapantsula', 'Vuvuzela', 'Ding Dong'.

Asiphindeleni to Codesa, but negotiating better terms. Terms that put the economic upliftment of black people at the centre of everything. Fok, asiphindeleni.

---

10   Twalatsa and vosho are dance moves.

Asiphindeleni to the moment when Chris Maroleng told André Visagie, 'Don't touch me on my studio!' We collectively laughed, cried, died and came back to life, and died laughing all over again.

Asiphindeleni to when it used to rain in Cape Town and Capetonians were insufferable. What? They still are? Even without water? Oh, well. Asiphindeleni to a Cape Town with rain, anyway.

Asiphindeleni to South Africa being crowned Rugby World Cup champions in 1995. White people have been so miserable for the past few years. Asiphindeleni for white people.

Serious. Silindeni (what are we waiting for)? Asiphindeleni.

Melusi
on Current Affairs

▼▲▼▲▼

South Africa is at a precipice. I love that word, precipice. I first encountered it in Geography at school and fell in love with it. It was the only thing about Geography I liked. But I digress.

There are so many important things taking place in South Africa right now. Things that will shape the kind of country we will be going forward. It is important not to sleepwalk through this period. We all need to be fully present, playing our part however we can.

In this section, I share my thoughts on some of the events and issues of our times.

INKOMO

Inkomo is a cow. The plural of inkomo is izinkomo.

The cow is very important in Zulu culture, because it's a source of food, its hide can be used for various purposes, and it's a form of currency. To this day, there are actual instances where the value of some things is calculated in izinkomo. You then have to convert it into rands.

Inkomo is also the word for a person (or group of people) who is (or are) particularly bad at something. In the beginning, it just referred to people who sucked at soccer because they were as useful as a cow on the soccer field. Bafana Bafana and Orlando Pirates are the archetypes of this kind of soccer player.

However, there are also several other applications of this meaning of the word.

For instance, you can be inkomo at running a state-owned enterprise. So, so many of them.

Inkomo at being the head of the NPA: we all know him.

Inkomo at being president: you know who.

Inkomo at not being a racist prick: you know who you are.

Inkomo at reconciliation: you know who you are.

Inkomo at not having smallanyana skeletons: Bathabile and the ANC NEC.

You can be inkomo at fatherhood. Guys, this thing is hard, but we must keep working at it.

Inkomo at marriage: eish.

Inkomo at peeing into the toilet bowl: some men.

Inkomo at fashion: me.

Inkomo at respecting traffic lights: inner city pedestrians.

Inkomo at rain: Cape Town clouds.

Inkomo at driving: taxi drivers.

Inkomo at honesty: politicians.

You can be inkomo at sleeping: insomniacs.

Inkomo at humility: rappers.

Inkomo at wiping your own ass: toddlers.

Government is full of izinkomo at service delivery.

Corporate South Africa is izinkomo at transformation.

You can be inkomo at anything – sex, dancing, your job, school, whatever – but you don't have to remain one. Work at whatever it is you're doing. Practise. Read up on it. Learn from those who are better at it than you.

But most importantly, you have to want to get better at it.

NONKE

Nonke means all of you.

The word nonke was made infamous by DJ Euphonik, a club and radio DJ, when he used it to swear at his Twitter detractors. He made sure his detractors knew he was swearing at all of them, not just a few, by punctuating his statement with 'nonke'.

The word holds a special place in South Africans' hearts. When you say #nonke to a group of people, they know you're telling them to piss off, without your actually saying the words.

I wish I had the opportunity to meet a Gupta so that, when he introduces himself ('Hi, I am Atul.') I can respond by saying, 'Nonke!'

To the racists: #nonke

To the sexists: #nonke

To the xenophobes: #nonke

To the homophobes: #nonke

To the thieves: #nonke

To the corrupt: #nonke

To Bafana Bafana: #nonke

To estate trustees: #nonke

To banks: #nonke

To taxi drivers: #nonke

I could go on and on, but you get the gist.

THAKATHA

Thakatha is to bewitch.

It kind of sounds like the name of that one Gupta company, right? (In case you've been holed up in a cave, the company is Tegeta.) Well, I don't think it's a coincidence that the Guptas chose a name that sounds like thakatha. Tegeta seems to have completely bewitched Eskom and government employees.

How else do you explain what has been going down at Eskom? It was witchcraft (ubuthakathi). If you have been following the Eskom scandal closely, you'll know that witchcraft is the only thing that makes sense. Yes, there was greed, but there was also witchcraft at play.

After all, why would a grown man go on TV, talk about non-existent shebeens, cry like a baby, not know whether he resigned or retired, and then take pension money he knows he doesn't deserve? This is an educated man who's had a stellar career. Ubuthakathi by Tegeta.

How did Matshela Koko sit in front of the parliamentary committee and talk out of his ass? As he was talking, I was watching, thinking, *Whose father is this? It's not like your lies are going to hide anything, sir. The paper trail is there. Just admit what you've done. Make a plea deal or something.*

It's ubuthakathi that he was digging in his heels. It's Tegeta witchcraft.

Then there was Anoj Singh. Oh, Mr Singh. As the former Eskom chief financial officer explained his Dubai exploits, you could hear that this was a man othakathiwe (who has been bewitched) by Tegeta. You could even see Pravin thinking, *This bra is under some kind of spell. Indian bra to Indian bra,*

71

I know when Indians have bewitched another Indian. They've done a number on this idiot.

These Guptas abathakathi (are witches, the singular is um'-thakathi).

ULWAZI and UKWAZI

Ulwazi is 'knowledge', while ukwazi is 'to know' and 'ability (know-how)'. Sifuna ukwazi is 'we want to know', 'we want answers' and 'we want know-how'. Sifuna ulwazi is 'we want knowledge'.

In light of the fact that, as a nation, we continually have to deal with so many lies, these are important words and phrases. As a country, we're suffering from a severe case of lie-steriosis and we've had enough. We need ukwazi. We need ulwazi. Sifuna ukwazi. Sifuna ulwazi. They can't keep us in the dark any more. We won't have it.

Woolies lied to us with their cold meats that pretended to have gone to private school when they are no better than those you buy at Cambridge Food. Sifuna ukwazi. What else are they lying to us about? Is the butter chicken basted in butter or Holsum? Sifuna ukwazi.

Why are their stores so cold? Did they work out that extreme cold makes shoppers stupid? Sifuna ukwazi.

Ulwazi will be ours. Ukwazi is our right.

Who else was sourcing their house-brand cold meats from Enterprise? Food Lovers, talk to us. Sifuna ukwazi.

Restaurants and hotels were eerily silent during the listeriosis outbreak. We wanted them to talk us. Sandwich Baron? Hot Dog Café? Debonairs Pizza? We want ulwazi. Ukwazi is our right.

Schools? Talk to us. What have your tuck shops been serving our kids? Sifuna ukwazi. Speaking of schools, do you get a cut from your extortionist uniform supply partners? Would the schools supply mafia come after us if we decided to make our kids' uniforms ourselves? Sifuna ukwazi.

As the people of South Africa, we demand ukwazi. Too much is kept in the dark. Ulwazi is our right.

IQINISO

Iqiniso is truth.

When iqiniso came out that polony was the culprit in the listeriosis outbreak, no one was surprised. Even polony was like, 'Yeah, it was me. I did it.'

One day, we'll look back and realise all our problems, as a nation, are polony-based. All of them. And that's iqiniso.

LAMBILE

Lambile is 'hungry'. The root word is lamba (hunger / hungry).

We all know the proverb 'a lambile man is an angry man'. Well, it's actually 'a hungry man is an angry man'. That's me. Some people need coffee to feel human, before they start their day. Others need food. Caffeine is stupid.

The anger that comes with hunger is real. English speakers call it hangry, and it is why I don't trust people who fast. Lambile by choice? You cannot be trusted.

For a big portion of my high school years, I went to school with Muslim kids. I'd avoid them during Ramadan: they were always pissed off. Funny thing is, the smokers would keep smoking. I always thought that was cheating, but I'd never tell them. A teenager olambile (who is hungry) is even angrier than a man olambile.

Unfortunately, the world is teeming with hungry young people. This is dangerous. Very dangerous.

People balambile (are hungry). People are very hangry. The world cannot continue to function as it always has. The rich cannot continue to get richer while others starve. It cannot work. It will not work.

Those who seek to preserve the status quo are extremely naïve. People balambile and the status quo is the reason. As a nation, silambile (we are hungry) because of the status quo.

To paraphrase: abalambile (the hungry) will eat the rich. Most of the rich look like they'd taste awful, though. But not Beyoncé. She'd go well with some fava beans and a nice chianti. I call dibs on her.

UMHLABA

Umhlaba is 'land' and 'world'. Here is an excellent example of its use as the word for land: if aliens came to Afrika and found us bickering about whose umhlaba this is, and they decided to intervene, Afrikaners would get the whole continent.

ALIEN: Who are you?

AFRICANS: I am Herero. I am um'Zulu. Ke moTswana. I am Swahili, etc.

AFRIKANER: Ek is Afrikaans.

ALIEN: Well, then, Afrika goes to the Afrikaner.

Sneaky, sneaky.

There is a playful isiZulu expression that says 'umhlaba uyahlaba' (the world is a prickly place). Isn't it just. Hlaba is to prick.

The word umhlaba is not related to hlaba but to isihlabathi – sand.

UMLANDO

Umlando is history. With South Africa's messed-up history, there are so many things I wish had worked out differently. Take mining, for instance. Imagine what modern-day mining in South Africa would have looked like had things started off like this:

African landowner (let's call him Melusi) is chilling and minding his own business when settler dude (Jan) shows up.

JAN: Wassup, Mel?

MELUSI: WTF, man? I keep telling people to not call me Mel.

JAN: Sorry, Melus.

MELUSI: Fuuuuuuuuuuuuuuuuck. It's Melusi! There's an 'i' after the 's'. It's not like I'm Gwinyitshe, Kgomotso, Dlangamandla or Lodewikus. How are you getting 'Melusi' wrong? You know what, just leave it. Call me Sir.

JAN: Cool, but you're so sensitive, Sir.

MELUSI: Hou jou bek, Jan van Stinkbek. What's up?

JAN: Homie, let me holler at you about the land.

MELUSI: What about the land?

JAN: It's rich as hell, B. Full of bomb-ass minerals, precious stones and all this other dope shit.

MELUSI: Yes, and?

JAN: Well, I want in on some of that action.

MELUSI: Deez nuts.

JAN: Come on, homes. Hear me out. You'll dig what I have to say. I swears on the tribal tattoos of my unborn Fourways cage-fighter descendants.

MELUSI: I doubt it. I know your type.

JAN: Daymn, that's harsh, Sir.

MELUSI: All right, sorry. I'm listening.

JAN: Okay, so check it out. You gots the awesome land and I gots the awesome new mining techniques and machinery.

MELUSI: Right.

JAN: So let's go halvies on this bitch. As owner of the land and provider of the labour, you gets fifty per cent. As the dude with the new techniques, machines and new markets, I gets fifty per cent.

MELUSI: Ma nigga. I like how you get down. But we go sixty–forty. Sixty to me, forty to you.

JAN: But why sixty–forty?

MELUSI: Coz, 'tsek!

JAN: Fine. Sixty–forty ke. So, you're down?

MELUSI: Yeah, I'm in. I've just gotta run this by my people and see how they wanna do it. I'm no one-man show.

JAN: Yeah, I get it. Do your thing, my ni—

MELUSI: Say it and I will kick you in your *Dromedaris*.

JAN: Sorry, Sir.

After consulting with his people and arriving at a plan that would benefit everyone and ensure that the land is not damaged by crap like acid mine drainage problems, Melusi returns to Jan and confirms it's on. They decide to celebrate.

MELUSI: Let's go jam to some deep house tunes.

JAN: Oh, yeah!

MELUSI: Good times!

JAN: So, you'll hook me up with some of your fine, big-booty, Afro honeys?

MELUSI: WTF? They're not my honeys. I don't know what kind of backward place you're from, but here everybody is their own person. So, when you see a woman you dig, you roll up to her and say what you gotta say. And make sure she's okay with you stepping up to her.

JAN: I hear you, Sir.

MELUSI: I gotta warn you, though – they don't call it afro-dizziac for nothin', man. You're gonna lose your damn mind and never go back home. Don't say you weren't warned.

And they lived happily ever after.

Until Jan started eyeing Melusi's sugar cane eThekwini.

I don't know why they would be speaking in American street vernacular, but they would.

ISIFO

In early 2018, South Africa was in the grips of listeria hysteria, and rightly so. It was a disaster, especially for kota-consuming[11] communities and their corresponding kota-based economies, since cold meats were the source of the virus. No cold meats; no kota.

---

11 Kota means quarter, but is also a fast food item consisting of a quarter of a loaf of bread with fillings that could include cold meats.

Looking back at that period when disease and death were unexpectedly top of mind brings us to the isiZulu word isifo. Because abeZulu are extremists, isifo means both 'disease' and 'a death'. Not 'death': 'a death'.

If you're sick, unesifo (une = you have). If there's been a death in the family, kunesifo (kune = there is). The death does not need to have been because of disease. The word is related to fa, the isiZulu word for 'die'.

Now, please don't tell any of this to Aunty Helen Dudu-Zille. She'll immediately tweet that isifo means both 'disease' and 'a death' because, before there was the awesomeness that was colonialism, black people had no knowledge of medicine, so, when one fell ill, one was doomed to die, regardless of the type of illness they had contracted.

Dudu-Zille is the kind of aunty who takes morbid joy from relatives' misfortune and likes putting everyone down. We all have a toxic Aunty Dudu-Zille. If you think you don't have one, but you live in the Western Cape, you're wrong. Infectious diseases are enough of a crisis without that aunty piling on the misery.

Now back to isifo called listeriosis. It has not been eliminated and will never be. It just needs to be contained.

If you suspect you've eaten contaminated food, please don't be fooled into thinking that gargling with Listerine will save you. You will still die. You'll have minty, fresh breath, but you will die. Fresh breath is wasted on a corpse. There will be isifo in the family from this sifo.

PS: White person, your daughter's boyfriend is Sipho, not Sifo. You've been insulting him all these years. Or maybe you were doing so intentionally, Aunty Dudu-Zille.

IMVULA

Imvula is rain. What a special thing, a true blessing. It nourishes the earth, cools us down, provides water for beer and is said to be a symbolic washing away of our troubles.

Mvula is related to vula, the isiZulu word for 'open'. It's the skies opening up, talking about feelings and crying like a little baby.

But nooo, not Cape Town's sky. Cape Town's sky is one crazy motherf*^^$# – part Xhosa, part gangster, part Afrikaner. The Cape Town sky is not some nkwenkwe (boy). It's been to the mountain and came back a real man, dammit. And real men don't cry. In fact, now that it's been to the mountain, you must wait on it hand and foot, woman, even though it's completely useless to you.

The Cape Town sky is a Hard Livings, a Sexy Boy and a 28, combined. You can dala[12] if you must, but it won't skrik or shed a single tear. It's a boer and has no time for you soft, entitled lot. Life is tough; get tougher. With its perfect tan, manicured nails, French perfume and designer shades, it sips champagne, unfazed by your suffering, pleb. If you weren't so lazy, you could also make something of yourself, it tells you.

The Cape Town sky has problems, man. Big problems.

Hey, I'm not mocking you, Cape Town. We all wish you a kinder sky that showers you with lots of imvula and love. I am always willing to drive down there, wash my car and – voilà – you'll have rain. I know this because every time I wash my car Jozi's sensitive sky takes one look at my shiny ride and is brought to tears. Joburg sky, you softy, you.

---

12 See 'Dala', p. 57.

Cape Town, maybe you can take Nomvula Mokonyane? Her name means 'she of the rain'. She who once threatened to protect number 1, with her number 2 maker. I wonder, is that why they made her Minister of Water and Sanitation?

No, don't want her? I figured as much.

LOVA

This word is dedicated to the legends who take 'sick leave' on Fridays and Mondays. We see you. We know what you're up to. Salute.

Lova is related to the English word 'loaf'. Not loaf of bread or meat loaf. Lova is 'to loaf', as in the verb.

To lova is to bunk, as in bunking work or school. South Africans love to lova.

The word is also used to describe an unemployed person – ulova. If you're loafing around the neighbourhood because you don't have a job or don't go to school, you are ulova – a loafer.

Ulova is also a term of endearment, used mostly by men towards one another. If a guy calls you ulova, it doesn't mean he thinks you're unemployed. He's just saying, 'Hey, buddy.'

Obviously, if someone sends you a text that says 'Hey, lova', it can be confusing. Are you hitting on me? What do you want? Leave me alone.

Some people can lova even though they are physically at work. Parliament, local government, City of Cape Town water management task team, some Home Affairs offices, some traffic department offices, previous ANC NECs – so much loving.

On a serious note, though, Productivity South Africa says we are a nation of olovas (plural), and that is not good at all. We need to get off our asses and get working.

WOZA

Woza means come.

The word is an invitation. In a country with one of the world's highest inequality gaps and where society is gripped by numerous tensions, uncertainty and divisions, we need to be using this word more. We need to open our hearts and invite more people in and share our lives, opportunities, knowledge and bread with fellow South Africans.

Woza also speaks to a type of witchcraft that keeps you coming back for more. This is called woza-woza. It's a mythical potion.

Chicken Licken Hotwings have woza-woza.

You keep going back to your nonsense ex because her daai ding has woza-woza.

During Mr Zuma's time as head of the ANC, the ANC NEC was powerless against his woza-woza.

In business and in your career, you need to have woza-woza so you become indispensable to your clients, customers, employers and colleagues. You gain that kind of woza-woza from consistently delivering exceptional value.

Obviously, we also have to mention woza's use as an exclamation, signalling extreme enjoyment. Woza nawe! A party ain't a party unless everyone is having a good time.

ISIMO

Isimo is a situation or a state.

The state (isimo) we've found ourselves in over the past ten years or so has been pathetic. We've had no idea whether we are coming or going. We've been paralysed.

You've seen the Men's Clinic ads. Yup, it's bad. And, no, I am not saying anything about myself and umshini wami.

The real problem is that we don't have a common goal. We are all pulling in different directions. This has to stop. The only way this will happen is if we decide what we're about and pursue it aggressively. I am not talking about airy-fairy ubuntu-and-rainbow-nation sappiness. We're not going to hug one another out of poverty.

We need something tangible. Like the Germans are known for engineering and the Swiss for chocolate, watch-making and cheese – we need something like that.

I say we go with dance music. Yup, house music, gqom et al will save us.

We already produce this type of music in staggering quantities and at mind-boggling rates. South Africa is a nation of bedroom producers and we are damn good at this dance music thing. In fact, we're so good that, in 2015, South Africa won Dance Nation of The Year at the DJ Awards in Ibiza. Now, imagine if we were deliberate about it.

Isimo of our economy would change.

Some kids could study to be pharmaceutical scientists so they can invent new, awesome drugs to take at dance music festivals. Other kids could study to be doctors to save the ones who'd OD'd on the awesome drugs.

We'd also need cops to arrest the ones dealing the awesome drugs and prosecutors to prosecute the purveyors of the drugs. Some kids might want to become defence lawyers to help the drug dealers.

Tech entrepreneurs would disrupt the funeral industry with Uber-like services. When you drop dead from the drugs, the hearse knows exactly where to pick you up. Yes, kids, drugs kill.

The insurance industry would boom.

Construction of new venues would boost the economy.

Dance tourism would be awesome. We could even create our own cryptocurrency – BeatCoin. Any career you can think of would be geared towards making us the best at this dance music thing. Come on, guys, let's rally around dance music and change our country's isimo.

We've already got the likes of Black Coffee doing our bidding internationally. And, if it doesn't work out, at least we'll have tons of dope tunes to get down to.

ISISU

Isisu is 'stomach' or 'belly'. Isisu is the source of so much trouble. It overrides the brain, and even the soul. It's often responsible for so many bad decisions.

A sisu decision you can always smell a mile away.

Did the mayor give his wife a city contract? Now that's a sisu call.

Another city gives the company of a former ambassador to Argentina a contract to tell people there is no water. Yes, another sisu decision.

Black First Land First. That's an unkempt man's sisu decision.

Is your marriage a sisu decision? Are you staying because of isisu? Or are you leaving because of isisu?

Are you in a sisu friendship? Is it your sisu or the other person's that's at play?

How much of your life is being ruled by your isisu? Isisu never gets full. The more you feed it, the more it wants. Want. Want. Want. It's insatiable and has given us things like:

Colonialism

Apartheid

Capitalism

Nationalism

State capture

Racism

Sexism

Glass ceilings

Human trafficking.

Of course, isisu is not all bad. Scientists say a gut feeling is a real thing because isisu is the second brain. I believe that and go with my isisu a lot of the time. Like when I was writing this – my isisu told me that this explanation was going to offend some people. Sorry, not sorry.

Isisu is also a euphemism for pregnancy.

IS'PILIYONI

Is'piliyoni is a colloquial isiZulu term for experience.

It's basically the English word 'experience', Zulufied. Zulu-fying happens when the Council for Giving isiZulu Names and Words to Foreign Words, Concepts and General Foreign Shit (CFGiZNAWTFWCAGFS) can't be bothered to give something an isiZulu name or word. They just take the foreign word and give it an isiZulu twist. Of course, experience is not a foreign concept, but the word 'experience' is foreign.

So, why does the CFGiZNAWTFWCAGFS sometimes Zulufy instead of giving things proper isiZulu words and names? Who knows. They are the CFGiZNAWTFWCAGFS and their inner workings are a mystery to the rest of us.

Of course, sometimes they Zulufy because they are busy with matters relating to Shembe or the King and they don't have time to apply themselves properly. Then there are the instances where they Zulufy because the thing being dealt with irritates them and they'd rather not waste their time and energy on it. That is the case with experience.

Experience has been, and continues to be, a real thorn in the side of countless job seekers, including abeZulu job seekers. And this upsets us. Many of our people remain unemployed because of experience – or, rather, their lack thereof. But how are people supposed to gain ispiliyoni if they are not given the opportunity to work? Is'piliyoni doesn't just happen, nje. It's not a weed.

You're probably also asking yourself how, in the Zulufying process, is'piliyoni ended up having an 'l', whereas experience has an 'r'. Why isn't it is'piriyoni? Well, if the CFGiZNAWTFW-CAGFS had left the 'r' in, they would not have done their Zulufying job properly because the letter 'r' is often replaced with an 'l' in isiZulu.

Seriously. Or, should I say, seliously. That is why our new president is called Silili, instead of Cyril.

Speaking of Silili, what is'piliyoni does he have of being a president? One moment he was a humble farmer, miner and fast-food worker, the next he is president. I guess this is'piliyoni requirement doesn't apply to all. Just kidding. Silili has enough is'piliyoni in politics and leadership. And he is going to need it. All of it.

Anyway, back to is'piliyoni. Please give people a chance to gain it. Don't just turn them away at the door. Set up learnerships and internships and make the workplace accessible. We beg you. We need to gain this is'piliyoni.

BTW, I have no idea why the 'nce' in 'experience' is not represented in 'is'piliyoni'. I don't know why it's not 'is'spiliyonsi'. You'll have to contact the CFGiZNAWTFWCAGFS directly for a firm answer.

IMVU

Imvu is sheep.

I remember the first time I saw the video of Nhlanhla Nene's chair breaking and him falling down. He fell without making a sound, not even a 'yoh'. I would have screamed, 'Yoh, Jesu. Yoh, ngiyafa! (I am dying!)' I watched that video again and again and eventually came to the following conclusion: 'This man imvu.'

Unlike a goat (imbuzi), imvu dies without screaming. When Mr Nene was fired from his post, again he went quietly. Some people think that's an honourable thing. I disagree. The bad people are counting on exactly this reaction. They want us to roll over and play dead.

Not a chance. As the African-American writer Zora Neale Hurston wrote, 'If you are silent about your pain, they'll kill you and say you enjoyed it.' (I've tried reading some of her work online but yoh, it's a tough read.)

In a society like ours, there can be no silent bystanders. Wherever you see injustice, corruption, criminality and unfairness, don't be imvu. Don't worry about abantu bazothini (what will people say) or usifakela amehlo (you're bringing us unwanted attention). The bad guys are not shy. They walk proudly with their apartheid flag. They loot, with impunity. They rob. They embezzle. They assault. And all of it takes place publicly because they expect us to be izimvu (sheep, plural – yes, English weirdos).

I am always amazed when I see videos of robbers with no masks or disguises on. How did we let it get to a point where the bad guys aren't even scared?

How did we get to a point where people were so comfortable about saying the kinds of things they'd say in the News24 comments section? It got so bad that News24 even had to turn off direct commenting. I used to imagine those people sitting at their computers in their undies, frothing at the mouth and pulling out clumps of hair. But the reality is it's probably your pretty colleague with the nice smile and a love for hip-hop. She luuuurves Cardi B.

Jerr, News24 comments were something else. How do people live with so much hate?

INGOMA

Ingoma is 'a song'.

I'd like to share a funny, but sad, story about ingoma.

While driving the kids to school one morning, I suggested we sing. The daughter started singing; all her songs were English nursery rhymes. So, I decided to counter that with isiZulu

87

songs from my youth. A few songs in, I realised I was just singing struggle songs.

What the hell kind of childhood did I have? Ya, neh.

The most poignant and sorrowful struggle song has always been 'Senzeni na?' It is a question: 'What have we done to deserve this?'

It asks, what have we done to have you treat us like this? Why are you killing us? Why are you displacing us, dispossessing us? What have we ever done to you?

It is beautiful and haunting. It's ingoma that really encapsulated the struggle.

To hear it being sung in earnest in this day and age because people are still being killed, are still poor, are still homeless and hungry, is heartbreaking.

Senzeni na?

UMBHEDO

Umbhedo is 'nonsense'.

Someone once asked me why black people don't condemn white farm murders. The question threw me off because black people do condemn white farm murders. When we cry about the high crime rates, white farmers, who've also been victims, are included. We just don't single those murders out: they are no more tragic than others. Maybe they are more tragic to some people because that is how they see the world – and because some lives hold more value to them than others?

(BTW, we don't have a nationwide WhatsApp group for black people where we discuss ways to ruin white people's lives. People need to get that umbhedo out of their heads.)

KHUZEKA

Khuzeka is related to the word khuza which means 'to reprimand', while khuzeka means 'to heed warnings/be reprimandable'.

This word exists because so many South Africans who should be reprimanded are not reprimandable. We continue to do as we like, despite reproaches, pleas and warnings. If more of us would khuzeka, so much would be achieved.

Racist, khuzeka. Seriously, you're boring.

BMW driver, khuzeka. Otherwise pappa wag vir jou.

Blesser, khuzeka. That's your kids' school fees you're blowing on grooming school kids for sex. Sies!

Gold digger, khuzeka. The man you're making out with used to bully your father in high school.

Taxi driver, khuzeka. You're endangering people's lives – your passengers', as well as fellow motorists'.

Apartheid denialist, khuzeka. Seriously. Stop it.

Orlando Pirates supporter, khuzeka. Your friends and family can't spend all their days comforting you.

Bafana Bafana, khuzekani (plural). You've caused us enough hurt.

False prophet, khuzeka. Our people have suffered enough.

Person who follows a false prophet, khuzeka. Surely you know Doom/petrol/antifreeze is not good for you.

Hairman Mashaba and your xenophobia, khuzeka. You've done worse things to us than any foreigner ever could. Perms, S-curls, finger waves, burnt scalps – we remember.

Toddler, khuzeka. Khuzeka, man.

Steve Hofmeyr, khuz— Never mind. I'm wasting my breath on this one.

ISHUBABA

Ishubaba is a burnt, dry, or scaly piece of skin, particularly on the face. The word is most often used in its plural form – amashubaba.

Ishubaba could be as a result of a skin condition, substance abuse or whatever the hell else. I bet the word has its roots in skin lightening treatment gone wrong (thanks again, colonialism), because when the lightening cream starts burning your face, you're likely to say, 'Shu, iyababa (Shoo, it burns).'

Due to their skin lightening roots, it's not a good thing to have amashubaba. It implies that you've been up to nonsense. If one moment you were fine, then boom! you have amashubaba, the words you are most likely to hear are, 'Bewenzani? (What were you doing?)' or 'Ulayekile (It serves you right).'

You can try to explain that it's a skin disease, but we don't believe you. Obviously, it could be a skin condition, we know that, but *you* have amashubaba because we know you and you must've been up to no good.

Some people have amashubaba on their hearts, souls, minds or brains. It manifests in fucked-up behaviour. Our former president has amashubaba on his heart. Why else would he have let things get this bad?

Big business is run by people who have amashubaba on their souls. Hello, Markus.

There is a premier in the Western Cape who doesn't know how to hide amashubaba on her brain.

Racists also have amashubaba in their heads.

Criminals are South Africa's biggest shubaba. Yes, not only do they have amashubaba on their hearts, souls, minds and brains, they are actually amashubaba themselves.

Besides criminals, there are other people and things that are amashubaba.

I have a neighbour who is the worst shubaba in my life.

Some people have exes who are amashubaba in their lives. Others have lovers who are amashubaba and they don't know how to get rid of them. Amashubaba don't just go away. Some never do.

Corruption is the ANC's shubaba.

DA's racists: amashubaba.

The EFF is teeming with amashubaba.

Shoo, South Africa has some serious shubabas to deal with. But I think we can win as long as we all work towards not being amashubaba ourselves.

IHLAYA

Ihlaya is 'a joke'. The plural is amahlaya.

Q: What did the female horse say to the male horse?

A: Do you wanna neigh?

That's ihlaya that is silly and childish. But silly, childish amahlaya have a place in society. We can't be serious all the time, especially when faced with the kind of serious challenges we have ahead of us as a nation. We have to laugh; if we don't, we'll spend all our time crying, and nobody likes a crybaby.

People can also be amahlaya. We've seen it with the leadership of the various political parties. But they are not funny at all, because they have been elected to their positions not to be a source of entertainment, but to deliver solutions. We have the Trevor Noahs of this world for entertainment.

Amahlaya can also reveal a society's temperature – not only

in the sort of amahlaya made, but also in who laughs at what. Amahlaya about land, gender, sexual orientation, political parties and xenophobia need to be approached with caution. Take this one for instance: A gay, EFF-supporting Nigerian walks into a bar in Orania …

Hahahaha. There is no such ihlaya! But shit, it would be funny to see a gay, EFF-supporting Nigerian walk into a bar in Orania. Especially if he's flamboyant and wearing the beret and T-shirt.

Anyway, a male horse is a stallion and a female a mare. I point this out because I know some people can't enjoy a silly hlaya without analysis paralysis, so they are still hung up on why I didn't use those terms in the hlaya at the start of this section. There – I have now put you out of your misery.

UKHAMISILE

Ukhamisile is related to the verb khamisa, to open your mouth. Ukhamisile is to have your mouth open.

It also means you are being useless, as in, 'Cyril, you are sitting there with your mouth wide open, doing nothing while the truth about Gigaba's lies is revealing itself.' Yeah, well, that's how many South Africans were feeling in early 2018, when the truth about Malusi Gigaba's lies about the South African citizenship of the Gupta family were coming out.

The open mouth could be because a person has been stunned or bamboozled, is aghast, or is just plain stupid or weak. No matter the reason, the net result is you are sitting there, paralysed, with your mouth open.

This term is a favourite with mothers, who use it right before they slap a teenager into action. Sometimes they say it and simultaneously thumela a hot klap because the klap is meant to close that stupid, gaping mouth. That slap can be followed by another one because the first one left you shocked, with your mouth open even wider, so it has to be closed with another slap on your other cheek. To avoid all this slapping, a teenager always has to look alive and be busy.

We should treat politicians and bureaucrats the same way. We should constantly be klapping them to ensure they don't just sit there with their mouths wide open, letting flies in and out, while the country burns, runs dry, or gets sucked dry.

Whenever you bump into one of these creatures, don't ask any questions. Just say, 'Ukhamisile!' followed by a hot klap. You might not be sure exactly where they are slacking, but they know. They also know they deserve the klap.

But we, as citizens, also need to be slapped because sikhamisile (we have our mouths wide open). People are living in atrocious conditions. The state of education is poor. The inequality gap is widening at an alarming rate. Households continue to abuse and underpay their helpers and gardeners. Cities are running dry. The majority of South Africans are landless. Crime is rampant. Women and children are violated. The state of health care is sickening. Racists and denialists are comfortable. Corporates are ripping us off and poisoning us. Bafana Bafana are not going to the World Cup. WhatsApp group admins are dictators. Sikhamisile.

Ukhamisile is 'your mouth is open' or 'his or her mouth is open', depending on the intonation.

Sikhamisile is 'our mouths are open'.

Bakhamisile is 'their mouths are open'.

Nikhamisile is 'your mouths are open'.

Melusi's Everyday Family

▼▲▼

Family is everything and my children are my inspiration. Having grown up without a father, it gives me great satisfaction and joy to be a present and involved dad.

But this parenting thing is not easy. I am not always sure I am doing it right. But since none of my children have disowned me, I will take it as a vote of confidence in my fatherhood.

Being a husband is also another thing I hope I'm doing right. The wife hasn't bolted; I'll take that as sign that it's all good. Well, I hope she's still around when you read this. Touch wood …

UMHLOLA

Umhlola means ridiculousness.

One time, I was dropping my daughter off at school when her teacher politely asked to speak with me. It seemed serious. What had Azande done? She is never in trouble.

It turned out it wasn't she who was in trouble …

TEACHER: Mr Tshabalala, we got a distressing message from one of the other kids' parents.

ME: What did Aza do?

TEACHER: It's not really Azande. It's you.

ME: Me? What did I do?

TEACHER: It's your views, sir.

ME: My views? My views on what?

TEACHER: You're an anti-Semite, sir.

ME: WTF, lady?

TEACHER: Please watch your language, Mr Tshabalala.

ME: I'm sorry about the language, but what are you talking about? Where did you get that?

TEACHER: Your daughter, Azande, told one of the other kids that you said Nazis are your favourite, that they are awesome.

ME: What?

TEACHER: That is what your daughter told her friend and the friend told her parents. The parents then contacted us.

ME: I said I like Nazis?

TEACHER: Yes, and that kind of ideology is not acceptable at this school.

ME: Of course it's not acceptable! It's not acceptable anywhere – my house included.

Seriously, what makes this woman believe I'd be into Nazis? Why would Nazis and I be on the same side?

ME: Can I talk to Azande? Aza!

TEACHER: No, Sir. Leave Azande out of this. She is just a baby.

(Azande arrives, smiling.)

AZANDE: Yes, Daddy?

ME: Nana, the teacher says I told you I like Nazis. When was this?

AZANDE: Yes, you did, Daddy.

ME: When? When did I say that?

AZANDE: When you came home with a box of oranges and said the oranges are not oranges. You said they are Nazis and you love them.

ME (doing a dance, all up in teach's face): Lady, she meant naartjies. I love naartjies. They *are* awesome.

TEACHER: Compose yourself, Mr Tshabalala.

ME: Whatever, teacher lady. I love naartjies!

AZANDE: Bye, Daddy.

ME: Bye, nana. Have a great day. I'll give you a naartjie later.

That was umhlola.

UMZALI

Umzali is a parent.

The root word of umzali is zala – birth. So, umzali is literally one who gives birth. It makes one feel like a baby-making factory.

With my first kid, I was in denial: 'One child does not make me a baby-making factory. You don't cook one meal and you're suddenly a chef.'

I have three, now. I'm a factory and should be charged a carbon tax.

Iya ocansini (have sex), they said. It'll be fun, they said. Oho.

The English word 'parent' is less accusatory, especially when your child has broken tomato sauce bottles at Pick n Pay and you've dashed off to hide in the detergents aisle. In English, they'll say, 'Where's the parent?' In isiZulu, it's, 'Uphi umzali wakhe?' which is 'Where is the breeder, who gave birth to her?' Come on, why must we call each other names, now?

But since I am not the one who actually gives birth, am I really umzali? Yeah, I am – there's no getting out of it.

A related word is umzala – cousin. Isn't that lovely. It's a constant reminder that your cousins are your blood. Even that one. Yes, you know which one.

Then you have mzalwane – born-again Christian. My mother is umzali and umzalwane. She'd love it if I were, too, but I am okay just being umzali and umzala.

Zala also relates to growth, as is the case with investments. Your money iyazala (gives birth to more money) and grows. That growth is called inzalo. Interest (whether investment or debt) is inzalo.

(BTW, I enjoy being umzali and adore my children.)

GCOBA

Gcoba is to spread or apply. As in, you spread butter and apply lotion.

Me (to the Tshabalala children): Revolution is the only way. We have to dismantle the system, topple the bourgeoisie and seize the means of production.

My five-year-old daughter: But we don't even use Revlon lotion. We use Vaseline.

Revolution will not take hold in the Tshabalala household for as long as people are more interested in what brand they gcoba than anything else.

IZINGANE

Izingane is children.

Izingane are beautiful souls. They'll say things they don't believe just to make you feel good, like 'Daddy, you're the smartest man in the world,' or 'Daddy, you're the handsomest man ever.'

But izingane don't give a shit about your hangover. Not *ever*.

Then, they want to interact with you. RIGHT. NOW.

UBABA/-BABA

Ubaba means father and baba means (spicy) hot.

I've never been into spicy food, but as ubaba, I have adapted to hot food so my children would stop wanting some of whatever I was eating. Sadly, they have since evolved to tolerate baba food.

NAKA

Naka means both to pay attention to and to bother someone.

Here is an example of how to use the word. You see your young daughter eating a slice of a yellow fruit and you're inspired to use the moment to teach her something interesting, so you say, 'Did you know that, as you're eating that pineapple, it's also eating you? The pineapple produces an enzyme that breaks down protein.'

The daughter turns to you, a bit annoyed, and responds, 'Daddy, I am eating a mango.'

Can you see which form of the word applies where?

THENGA

Thenga is to buy.

On my shopping list, the wife always includes the item 'fresh milk'. What other kind of milk would I thenga? The woman has no faith in me.

I suspect it's because I once came back with something called chard when I was meant to thenga spinach. She never regained her trust in my ability to thenga the right thing. But if it looks like spinach, it must be spinach. No?

She also once sent me to buy squash and I came back with Oros. She was not happy. But can you blame me? If you send me to buy a crap thing that shares a name with an awesome thing, I'm obviously going to buy the awesome thing. Wait until she sends me to thenga ithanga (ithanga is both thigh and pumpkin).

PHEKA

Pheka is to cook. Whenever I cook, my kids make sure to compliment my food. The wife's cooking is a million times better, but she gets no compliments. Why? Because they know she's a big girl and I'm fragile.

HLUKANISA

Hlukanisa means to differentiate between or separate. Separate as in, teenage boys exist to hlukanisa you and your money through groceries.

Seriously, though. Children will hlukanisa you and some of your most favoured things. It begins even before they are born.

The moment the woman falls pregnant, you swiftly start to part ways with the things you love. The first thing to go is your sanity.

I suspect losing stuff you care about because of kids never stops, until you die. It seems that, even when you're on your deathbed, they're discussing who gets what. What the hell?

If God really loved us the way the Bible claims, he would have kept procreation and sex separate. Hlukanisa them. Yes, yes, there are contraceptives, but we are only human.

SUZA

Suza is to fart or pass gas.

Because of the rampant child abuse in South Africa, I've encouraged my daughter to snitch about everything. It has backfired many times.

At the end of one parent–teacher evening, the teacher says the daughter mentioned I fart a lot. I tried to laugh it off, but this teacher proceeds to give me advice on how to deal with excessive gas – watch my diet blah, blah, blah. I wanted to die. This sort of meddling would never happen at a township school.

I did take the teacher's advice, though, and it did improve my situation drastically. However, that improvement damaged my relationship with my eldest son. Since I can no longer suza at will, we no longer have anything to talk about. I'd suza on his face, he'd scream, 'No, daddy! How could you?'

Then we'd laugh and laugh. Oh, what memorable times …

Now that's all gone. Thanks for nothing, nosy suburban teacher.

SHIDABA and CHAMA

Shidaba is to wipe one's butt after doing a number 2.

This is a very important thing in a civilised society. As such, people should only start eating solid food *after* they learn to shidaba. Yes, I am talking to you, toddlers and politicians.

Chama is to pee (urinate).

Speaking of peeing, I really hate unisex toilets. You walk into the loo and find that some asshole chama-ed[VII] all over the seat. Fortunately, because you pee standing, you can still do your business. But as you walk out, hoping to track down the culprit, a woman walks in and automatically assumes you're the pig. Argh.

And that's just at my house.

NUKA PHU!

Nuka phu! is an expression that describes a foul smell. Nuka is to smell. Phu indicates the extreme foulness of the smell. Whenever my teenage son and his friends hang out at the house on a hot day, ikhaya (home) linuka phu. Stinky buggers!

ASIMUFUNI

Asimufuni means 'we don't want him or her'.

No, this is not about Zuma, even though asimufuni.

It's not about NDZ either, even though asimufuni.

It also not about Helen Zille, even though asimufuni.

It's not even about Mmusi, even though asimufuni.

Hawu.

Is it about Steve Komphela, then? No, even though asimufuni.

Is it about Pieter Mulder? It could have been, but it isn't, even though asimufuni.

Is it about Kallie Kriel? No, even though asimufuni.

Is it about Steve Hofmeyr? No, it isn't, even though asimufuni.

Who is it about, then?

Is it about Katie Hopkins? It should be, but it isn't, even though asimufuni.

Is it about 'Captain KGB' Tshabalala? Nope, even though asimufuni.

Surely, it's about Tony Gupta. Surely. Look, uTony asimufuni, but this is not about him. It's also not about Atul, even though asimufuni. It's not about Rajesh, Varun or Prakash Gupta. There is a Prakash, right? No? Oh well, if there was, he'd know asimufuni.

This is not even about Markus Jooste, even though asimufuni. I'll tell you who this is about.

It's about another child – having one. Asimufuni. No, no, no. Asimufuni today. Asimufuni tomorrow. Asimufuni ever. The wife and I love the kids we have, but we do not, under any circumstances, want another one.

Asimufuni.

Fok.

UMNDENI

Umndeni is family.

You've got to love black families. In one umndeni, you can have people who speak all South African languages and more. It's daai intermarrying thing. Even if it means that you don't understand some of your nephews and nieces because they speak chiShona or Tshivenda.

Intra-mndeni tribalism and xenophobia are also a reality. Bring your Nigerian boyfriend home and you will see. Now he's accused of selling your cousin drugs.

Then your uncle doesn't talk to amaShangane and your other cousin is crying because her mother married umShangane. Then there's the lesbian rasta aunt. And the private school baby mama who'd rather be at Rockets Lolita's but has to be here because she's building a case for sole custody.

The youngest brother is a CEO somewhere and doesn't understand why these uneducated people are talking to him like this. He forgets that everyone's dreams had to take a back seat because the family believed in him. He thinks he made it on his own, so he votes DA.

Issa mess.

UFUZO

Ufuzo is 'a family trait'. It can be a physical, intellectual, emotional, personality, or any other kind of characteristic.

More often than not, it refers to the traits people don't want to take responsibility for. The problem is never poor parenting, poor diet or poor life choices. Nope, it's all ufuzo – and, of course, it originates from the other side of the family.

With South Africa's pervasive problem of broken families, ufuzo is used as an excuse with impunity because the other side too often can't defend themselves. I think that's why people go on that TV programme *Utatakho* – a show where people take paternity tests to find out who their real father is. It's because Sipho is looking to meet the father he's been told he inherited all his bullshit from.

You're a teenage drunkard: ufuzo. Ufuze (you take after) your useless dad.

Your milkshake brings all the boys to the yard (and I mean *all* the boys): ufuzo. Ufuze your useless father's skanky sisters.

You joined the DA: ufuzo. Ufuze your father's light-skinned father. You can't trust these light-skinned types. It's definitely the light-skinned ancestors' fault we got colonised.

You cry during sex: ufuzo. Again, it's the lighted-skinned men in your bloodline. They ruin everything.

You're in jail: ufuzo. Ufuze your father's mnyamane (very dark) brother. The mnyamanes get no love either.

You support Orlando Pirates: ufuzo. Ufuze your uncle who's been in jail since before you were born. He was also up to shit.

It gets really messed up if one of the parents is not um'Zulu. Then, the other parent's whole nation is blamed. You dropped out of medical school so you can slay with blessers – ufuzo. Ufuze lamaVenda wakubo (she takes after the Vendas).

Obviously, ufuzo applies to positive things, too, but everyone takes credit for those. The kid gets nine distinctions and even the neighbours are on some ufuze mina (she takes after me).

'Tsek.

Fun fact: If, at birth, the elders coo about the litany of ways in which the baby takes after you, they're trying to bamboozle you. That ain't your baby, son.

UMALUME

Umalume is uncle.

At the height of the listeriosis outbreak, a light was shone on the challenges of being a black malume: you're not allowed to eat the polony in the fridge because it's for the kids' skhaftins (school lunch), but fast forward a few years and umalume must run those same little shits' lobolo negotiations. That's so unfair.

MNSINSILA and KWAPHA

Mnsinsila is butt crack, while khwapha is armpit.

These two words always remind me of the misery of preparing to leave a wonderful holiday, heading back to the mnsinsila ka sathane (Satan's butt crack) that is Joburg, particularly Fourways. It's the Shoprite meat section of life.

Just thinking about it leaves the taste of a sweaty khwapha in my mouth. Don't ask me why I know what a sweaty armpit tastes like. You really don't want to know. But it is horrible and stays in your mouth for a really long time. You even taste it in your dreams.

Speaking of sweaty khwaphas, while we are by the seaside even my teenage son's armpits don't stink. My fellow Joburgers are probably thinking, *Jerr, buddy. You're umnsinsila ka sathane yourself, traitor!*

Okay, okay it's not our beloved Jozi that I'm not keen on. It's our little family getaways coming to an end. What a great time I always have with my wife and kids, bumming on the beach, exposing my ashy mnsinsila.

Sure, all my favourite people (mother, brother, cousins, aunts and friends) live in Joburg, but there is no beach, no soothing sound of crashing waves. No, just crippling heat, metro police and lots and lots of traffic on William Nicol – the devil's sweat duct.

I always miss the breezy coast, but I have to be in the city of gold to get my mnsinsila and khwapha sweaty as I dig for more of that gold. After all, family getaways don't pay for themselves.

I can already hear those The Parks types saying, 'But why don't you just leave Fourways?'

I can't. I love pain.

NSUNDU

Nsundu is 'brown'.

This word reminds me of the first time my wife sent me to buy brown rice and I came back with Tastic because it's in predominantly brown packaging. It turned out that's not what brown rice is. I tried to convince her to never send me to the shops again. I didn't succeed.

MONA

Mona is jealousy. Which is what I feel whenever my kids are on holiday and I have to go to work, especially in December. I know I should be happy for them, but that simply doesn't happen.

Why do they get to stay home while I still have to slave away? It's not fair. I hate them. I know I shouldn't be jealous of people who don't even know how to chew with their mouths closed. But I am.

I would swap lives with them in December, even if it meant going back to not being able to wipe my ass properly. Really, I would.

What, I'm wearing my shoes 'banana' (on the wrong feet)?

Yeah, well I'm at home and you're dealing with a jammed printer. I'd ride around on a bike with training wheels if it meant I get to stay at home all December.

I'll even embrace having my teenage son's pimples and wet dreams. Bring them on. I'd take having his smelly armpits in December and not care what you think.

You're going to be stuck in a meeting that should have been an e-mail, while I'm at home digging in my nose. That's what my youngest thinks as he waves me goodbye on a December morning. I see him mocking me with his eyes.

I would even take your kids' braces and Coke-bottle glasses if it meant we could swap lives. Your daughter is nine and still peeing her bed? I'll take it, any day.

Your son is six and still drinks from your breast? I'll gladly take his place, but first I need to see the packaging.

Your kid sticks toys up his butt? I have friends who swear by it.

Would I give up beer? Of course! Easy.

Would I give up sex? What? What's wrong with you, sadist?

ISINKWA

Isinkwa is bread.

Some time ago, my eldest son asked me what type of man I am. I had never thought about it. I just go about the business of each day, doing what I do. Some of it is important. Some of it is nonsense. Whatever.

However, his question forced me to pause and think. What kind of man *am* I? And why does it matter?

I did not have an answer for him. Even though he didn't realise it, he had shaken me to my core. I was hit with the stark realisation that the answer would probably define what kind of man he would become.

Do I want him to be like me (whatever that means)?

I think I do. Maybe a little. At least the good bits. But is that two per cent, or ninety-eight per cent?

Then it occurred to me that I felt a bit hungry and could do with a sandwich. Yes, I like isinkwa and a sandwich would have been great right then.

I turned to him, looked him deep in the eye and said, 'My boy, let me tell you what kind of man I am. I'm the kind that would like a sandwich, right now. And because we don't have isinkwa, I am the kind of man that gets in his car and goes to buy isinkwa.'

We got each other that day. We connected on a different plane, without much talking.

And that, all thanks to isinkwa.

Melusi
on Being a Grown-up

▼▲▼▲▼

Earlier, I mentioned that I turned forty while writing this book. The big four-oh was a big deal. Not because forty is the new twenty. It isn't. The random pains and high blood pressure pills are there to ensure you don't get that wrong. Forty is forty.

Don't get me wrong, I have nothing against growing up. Sure, I enjoyed my youth, and the idea of being a forty-year-old is daunting, but I'm glad I am where I am right now. This book and the Melusi's Everyday Zulu initiative came about because I was nearing forty. I suddenly had clarity of thought and purpose.

In this section, I touch on becoming an old fart.

ANGISE NANDABA

Angise nandaba means 'I no longer care' (angisena = I no longer have, ndaba = care[VIII]).

I used to stress about holding up the queue while putting change in my wallet. Angise nandaba. Everyone must simply wait until I'm done.

There are so many things I used to stress about, but now angise nandaba.

The need to be cool: angise nandaba. Whatever. Really.

Being out and about, painting the town red: angise nandaba. I ran out of red paint a long time ago.

People who make more money than me: angise nandaba.

Past mistakes: angise nandaba. I must move on.

Failure: angise nandaba. We fail, we learn.

What I don't have: angise nandaba. I am focused on cherishing what I do have.

What ifs: angise nandaba. I'm no longer into torturing myself. I have kids for that.

Rejection: angise nandaba. You can't live a small life because you're scared you might get rejected when you reach for your dreams.

Society's expectations: angise nandaba. Suck it, society. Suck it!

UKUTEFA

Ukutefa is being a crybaby.

As a big crybaby, I am a good example. At forty, I always used to get pissed off when the vendors at intersections called me uncle. It would almost bring me to tears. But after a shower one morning, I stood in front of our full-length mirror and thought, *Motherf*cker! The vendors are right. I am their uncle.*

The wife told me my sobbing is a turn-off. That's ukutefa, being a crybaby. When someone whines about something inconsequential, you say uyatefa.

CABANGA

Cabanga is to think.

This is something I do way too much of, and it gets me into a tailspin. I'll be having a beer, then boom! I find myself thinking, *Shit, did I take my blood pressure pill this morning? I don't think I did. Oh, God, this is how it ends. I am too young to die. No, I'm not. If I were young, I would not be on blood pressure medication. I'm old and I am gonna die. I hope I get another chance to tell my kids I love them. I love them so much. Wait ... I did take the pill! Shoo. At least, I won't die today. In fact, it's those little shits that'll be the end of me.*

SHELA

Shela is to ask someone out or court them. If it's not your thing, to shela can be pretty daunting.

A few years back, a friend of mine told me he was thinking of getting a divorce, so I reminded him that, if he did, he would have to go back to shelaring.[IX] He was never any good at it back in the day, even though it was seemingly less treacherous than it is these days.

Today's young girls are hectic with their million-rand Eskimo hair weaves, champagne, Gucci bags, red-soled shoes, gel-tipped nails, trips to Dubai and layers and layers of make-up. All paid for by you. Aneva.

The idea of going back to a life of shelaring scared my buddy straight. He and his wife went through counselling and they are happier than ever before.

But there is a certain type of man with an appetite for uku-shela. He has a thick skin. No matter how many girls turn him down or humiliate him, he just brushes it off and moves on to the next one. We'll call him a Shelington.

Of course, you've also got the kind who doesn't know the difference between ukushela and harassment. Shem.

When you're out with a Shelington, you just have to accept that he will bring tons of girls to your table or will send shooters to various girls at different tables. It's best to leave your card at home because when the bill comes, it's gonna be mighty high and Shelington is going to want to split it equally.

If most Shelingtons applied themselves to their careers or projects with the same passion as they apply themselves to ukushela, they could change the world ...

IPHUPHO

Iphupho is a dream.

Have you ever dreamt you were out drinking, but then decided to walk home because driving drunk is a terrible idea? Then got arrested for walking drunk? In the dream, they had a roadblock and everything and were breathalysing pedestrians.

Well, I have. WORST. IPHUPHO. EVER.

Phupha is to dream. Phupha also means to fade, or lose shine or colour.

PHUZA

Phuza is a simple enough word, but can get you into trouble, especially in the workplace.

As we all know, phuza is to drink. The noun is isiphuzo. This applies not only to drinking booze, but to the consumption of all liquids.

It has also come to mean 'screw up', because so many screw-ups are booze-related. If you get fired from your job, uphuze umsebenzi (you drank the job). If you get into a car accident, uphuze imoto (you drank your car).

But the trouble with phuza comes from its meaning in isiXhosa, the second-biggest language in South Africa. Imagine you're Gert from finance, who fought hard for the year-end function budget because you wanna get down to some 'Nkalakatha'. The big day finally arrives, and you head down to the party in the basement parking on some 'dzuuum. dzum dzum dzum dzuuum. dzum dzum dzum dzum dzum dzum, nkalakatha!' when you bump into a female colleague.

Excited, you shout, 'It's phuza o'clock! We're gonna phuza today. We're gonna phuza hard! Wooh! Bottoms up!'

The next moment our female colleague screams: 'Yhu, Human Resources, umlungu ufuna ukundi rape-isha (the white man is trying to rape me)! Yhu!'

Now uGert uphuze umsebenzi. He's lost his job, all because, in isiXhosa, phuza is kiss. Yup, in the colonies, Phuza Thursday means Kiss Thursday. What a sexual harassment trap.

Let's be careful out there and not phuza ourselves into trouble.

PHUZA BODY

We all know what phuza face is – the ravaged face of a habitual alcohol abuser. Phuza face is the s'botho's[13] badge of (dis)honour.

---

13 S'botho is someone who's let their love for alcohol ruin their looks and lives. You don't even have to ask whether they drink; it's written on their faces. There are some famous s'bothos, but I will not mention their names because I don't want to get sued.

Well, I'd like to introduce a new concept. Phuza body. We all know it exists, but we never talk about it. It must come out of the shadows.

No, you are not fat. You have phuza body. You can't live on booze and braais. No, you are not skinny. You have phuza body. You can't live on spirits alone. Eat something.

No, it's not your genetics. It's that phuza body. Booze will kill you.

I am not judging here, just introducing a new phrase and concept.

Phuza body sucks much more than phuza face because, unlike phuza face, it kills. That's why I've started running, and drinking less.

Say no to having phuza body.

PS: A drink is isiphuzo. Face is buso. Body is umzimba.

ISITHEMBU

Isithembu is polygamy. Niiiiiiiiice.

But is it really so nice? Sure, you get more boobies and more daai-dings. But also more talking. I bet there is soooooo much talking. More children. Bloody snot-nosed brats everywhere. More in-laws. Thixo. More shopping. More therapy. More aaaaaaaaaah!

Isithembu is only for the clinically insane. The clinically insane and the rich. Yeah, you need to be mega-rich and out of your damn mind to get into isithembu. Uphambene.

If you're poor, leave other children alone. Just sit in your corner. That's where I am. In my corner, with my poverty. Look at what under-budgeted isithembu made former president you-know-who do just to make ends meet.

Obviously, I am speaking from a man's perspective and have no idea why a woman would get into isithembu. Maybe women in isithembu are the kind who don't want an asshole focusing all his attention on them and bugging them. 'Go to your other wives, Sibiya. Jesus.'

Speaking of women in isithembu, do their periods sync? Jehova. Is menstrual sync actually a real thing, anyway? I was told about it, but then read it wasn't true.

If menstrual sync is real, then that's exactly how isithembu got out of hand. Some asshole sex maniac was unhappy about his wife getting her period, so he got another wife. The two wives then synced so he got another, and another, and yet another as they all synced.

Did isithembu start as an abaThembu thing? Does isithembu mean the way of abaThembu? Did they give us Madiba and polygamy? Even Walter Sisulu was um'Thembu from his mother's side.

However, these men were not polygamists. Maybe it's because it's damn near impossible to maintain even one wife while doing hard labour eRobben Island.

Wherever it came from, isithembu is quite a thing. And to the comrades fighting this good fight, we say aluta continua; better you than me.

'YAZ UZOFA

About two weeks before my fortieth birthday, I woke up motivated one morning and decided to go for a run. Well, a few minutes into my run, my legs were burning and I could hear God laughing. When I realised I didn't have my phone on me, so I couldn't even Uber back home, I stopped, propped my hands on my knees and said to myself, "Yaz uzofa.'

'Yaz uzofa is shorthand for the rhetorical question, uyazi na ukuthi uzofa? (are you aware that you're going to die?). As you might have noticed, while the longer version is a question, 'uyaz uzofa' isn't. That's because uyaz uzofa is a statement, used to inform someone that they're being stupid, ridiculous, ungovernable and even deliciously delinquent.

We take it all the way to death because people don't listen, asakhuzeki (we don't listen when reprimanded). In my case, it related to the stupidity of thinking I could undo decades of hard living in under two weeks.

'Yaz uzofa is therefore often used when someone has done or said something they derive guilty pleasure from. In this context, it intends to convey that God will smite them.

When the former president first tried to read numbers on TV and my wife burst out laughing, I said, "Yaz uzofa, babes.'

When Julius Malema called Lindiwe Mazibuko a tea girl, everyone said, "Yaz uzofa.'

When the EFF's Mbuyiseni Ndlozi called the minister of international relations a sleepist in Parliament, the nation exclaimed, "Yaz uzofa.'

When that kid stole the Rolls-Royce and drove it to Riverlea, social media said, "Yaz uzofa.'

When Julius Malema called the president baba ka Duduzane, we all said, "Yaz uzofa.'

When Bathabile said the ANC NEC had smallanyana skeletons, members of the NEC said, "Yaz uzofa.'

When my six-year-old said, 'Daddy, your tummy is getting big,' I told her, "Yaz uzofa.'

When Julius Malema told the deputy speaker of Parliament to withdraw delela (disrespect), everybody said, "Yaz uzofa.'

Actually, why is Julius still alive? If God really smote people for being out of order, he would have sorted Julius out a long time ago. Does God even smite people any more? Does she even exist? Now, I am not saying Julius should die, but I bet if I taunted people the way he does, God would have dealt with me a long time ago.

(BTW, 'yaz uzofa also highlights how often we drop vowels when speaking. It's actually meant to be uyazi uzofa. If you don't speak the language, you'll end up thinking the word is 'yaz, instead of uyazi.)

UKWABELANA

Ukwabelana is sharing. The root word is kwaba (share).

I remember a conversation in which my six-year-old daughter was telling me about ukwabelana. She broke it down thus: 'When you care, you share. If you have something, you have to cut it into halves and give some to everybody. But their halves mustn't be too big because this is your thing, so you must still get the biggest piece.'

I should have followed these wise words in past business and personal relationships.

HLULA

Hlula means to defeat or beat.

There are many things that hlula me. So many. Some have been at it since I was a kid. Take math, for instance. No, I did not say take meth. Put that pipe down, skollie.

While doing his geometry homework, my son asked me to help him with a question that asked him to name four kinds of rays. There is no way that one would hlula me. I mean, that's easy – Ray Phiri, Ray Donovan, Ray Liotta and D-Ray.

UMCIMBI

Umcimbi is a celebration – a party.

I was once at some child's birthday party (I was dragged there kicking and screaming), and this slick four-year-old was there. For a split second, I was jealous that even he dressed better than me. Then I remembered he didn't have a bond, car instalments or school fees to pay, so he could afford to have fancy clothes. Nx.

I wonder where he is now. I hope he now has a bond, car instalments and school fees to pay. I hope there are no more mcimbis and fancy clothes for him – just bills. But since he was four only two years ago, all that is highly unlikely. His life is probably still one mcimbi after another. Lucky, lucky, well-dressed bastard.

PHUNYUKA

Phunyuka is to escape.

You arrive home, preoccupied with a problem you have to solve before tomorrow morning. In between playing with the kids and doing other daddy stuff, you crack a massive idea.

The next morning, the solution has survived the overnight test. In fact, it seems even better. As you mull it over while driving to the meeting, it doesn't lose any of its shine.

You walk into the boardroom with a bounce in your step and immediately your positive vibe is infectious. You start speaking, and they hang onto your every word. They love you. They really, really love you.

But then, mid-sentence, you realise you're talking shit. This idea is embarrassingly bad. It's literally the worst idea in history. A pile of crap. The others haven't noticed yet, but you now know it stinks. And they, too, will soon realise it.

You start to stumble over your words. The confidence is gone.

A concerned colleague asks, 'Syfo, are you okay, bud?'

This is your gap: 'What the hell, man? How many damn times must I tell you my name is not Syfo? I'm Sipho. Sipho Mkhwanazi. None of this Makhawanawazi rubbish either! I'm tired of lekaka!'

You toss shit across the room and storm out.

Phew, got out of that one. Now all they'll think is that you're just another overly sensitive darkie.

IGUGU

No, it's not the sound of the gqom drum, pumping out of a criminally loud Durban taxi. Igugu is something of value – your pride and joy. My children, for instance. There are other things I value, too, but nothing comes close to my kids.

Everybody has something that is igugu to them. Some are obvious choices like cars, property, qualifications, or a career, while others are strange, like a particular brand of sneakers. Yes, Jordan freaks, you're weirdos.

We're obviously discouraged from placing too much value

on earthly possessions, which is why the most popular funeral song ('Amagugu') is all about how earthly pride and joy remain on earth while you go to your grave alone. Talk about a double whammy. You are already sad that you're burying your friend, now you have to sing a song that shits on everything you love. No, man.

The song is always kicked off by the elder who tried to get your attention so you could give her a lift to the cemetery and you pretended not to see her. You avoided her because, if she's in your car, she's gonna corner you about why you don't come to church any more. She'll talk about what a good Sunday school boy you were, while the truth is you were always a delinquent, leading the other kids astray, convincing them to steal collection money because you knew the elders were embezzling it anyway.

When the elder kicks off 'Amagugu', she's looking you dead in the eye while gesticulating as if she's controlling a steering wheel and running a finger across her throat. Okay, I exaggerate, but she definitely wants you to know the song is about you and your precious luxury, a German car. It's as if she's cursing you, wishing you all kinds of ill.

That's *so* unChristian, gogo ka Thandi (Thandi's grandma). *So* unChristian. Ah, Thandi, she was igugu lakho (your pride and joy), until she fell pregnant with Nkululeko's baby. Look at them now. He's in prison and she has four kids, with four different guys.

You see, even though school wasn't igugu to you, you had enough sense to know that you need to stick it out and finish in order to have any kind of decent life and get the things you want like a luxury German sedan. On the other hand, Thandi focused on being pretty and popular, while Nkululeko just wanted the fast life, cutting corners wherever he could. Shem. Maybe I should visit him in prison. Not! I bet prison sucks so much.

Amagugu is the plural of igugu.

Lakho is your or yours.

UBHUTI

This word goes to the heart of masculinity, family dynamics, community relations, workplace dynamics, street politics, dating, authority and many other kinds of potential pitfalls a (Zulu) man has to navigate in twenty-first-century Africa. Issa mess.

While ubhuti should be a simple enough word to navigate, it is in fact a minefield, because it speaks to hierarchy and the issue of respect.

Family dynamics: Let's start with ubhuti as a word that refers to an older brother. All older brothers should be ubhuti, as in uBhut' Melusi, uBhut' Nhlanhla, uBhut' Whatever. But younger siblings are shitheads, so they pick and choose when to call their older brothers ubhuti. It's mostly when they need something important, like money or a kidney. If you're unemployed and aren't a match for organ donation, forget it – no ubhuti for you.

When you're all still kids, younger siblings also tend to start calling you ubhuti right after they got smacked by the local bully. Why? Because you are now supposed to go and avenge them. When the bully proceeds to beat your ass, too, you immediately lose your ubhuti status.

Community relations: Ubhuti is meant to be any man who

is older than you, but not old enough to be called umalume or ubaba. I once called a man ubhuti and my mother nearly lost it. 'Do you honestly think I could have a child his age? You must call this man umalume. Uyangi gugisa (you're ageing me)!'

There are older men who will insist on being called ubhuti when they are clearly umalume or ubaba. They usually try this with younger women in conversations that go something like this:

YOUNG WOMAN: Sorry, Malum' Thando.

OLDER GUY: You can call me uBhut' T.

YOUNG WOMAN: Hayi, Malum' Thando.

Then you get some useless guys who introduce themselves as ubhuti in an effort to impose their seniority. They usually try this on younger guys.

(Slightly) older guy: Hi, I'm uBhut' Thando.

Younger guy: Eita, Thando.

Workplace dynamics: Some people think they can bring their bhutitude (ubhuti attitude) to work. GTFOH,[14] the kids ain't having it. There is no ubhuti here. You're just Thami from Sales and 'tsek. But during disciplinary hearings, Xolani in HR is very much ubhuti …

Street politics: The guy with the most money is ubhuti, regardless of his age. In this day and age, even the guy with the cellphone charger can be ubhuti.

The dating scene: Thixo! What a mess. When some girls have ubhuti they think he is also their boyfriend's older brother and therefore he would have a say over the boyfriend. LOL. Whatever. He's just uJabu nge kiss-kiss (Jabu with knock-knees).

---

14 Get the fuck out of here.

We all know of the friend zone, but there's also a ubhuti zone. When a girl says you're like an older brother and starts calling you uBhut' Sthembiso, you've been ubhuti-zoned, Sthembiso! On the other hand, you do find relationships where the women refer to their boyfriends as ubhuti.

Authority: As with Xolani from HR, when you are in trouble with any form of authority and you're entirely in the wrong, the authority figure is always ubhuti, regardless of age.

Bonus: Ubhuti is also a term of endearment. When people are impressed with something you're doing, wearing, saying, etc., they'll refer to you as uBhuti. For instance, lobhutu uyang'chaza (this man is impressive).

Ubhuti is also used to indicate certain quirks or predilections. It loosely means boss of or king of something.

Ubhut' maswidi (sweets) and ubhut' madlisa both mean sugar daddy.

Ubhut' majaivane (a dancer) would be a guy who likes dancing.

Ubhut' mafinyela (to snort) would be a guy with a consistently runny nose.

Ubhut' woku phapha would be a tjatjarag guy.

In this way, it can be applied to almost any other word to indicate a quirk or predilection.

Melusi's Musings

▼▲▼▲▼

My mind wanders a lot. It always has. Weird, random thoughts fly in and out of it.

Some are sparked by events taking place around me, online or in the media. Others come out of nowhere and catch me off guard. I suspect we're all like that, though. Our brains have a life of their own and like to keep us entertained.

In this section, I share some weird and wonderful random thoughts.

IMBIZA

Imbiza is a pot. But it's also a herb. Most importantly, imbiza is a magical, all-in-one cure for all manner of ailments.

If it weren't for imbiza, abeZulu would not be such awesome taxi drivers or security guards. Do you think we would have been able to give South Africa its best president ever if it weren't for imbiza? Never. A concoction of herbs and the tears of Silili's supporters helps to make imbiza legendary. Seriously, if you're not using imbiza, there's no way you're ever going to live your best life. As our Sesotho-speaking friends would say, 'Ke makgona tsohle (Cure for alles)'.

You need to 'gain complexion'? Drink imbiza.

You want a tan, without risking skin cancer? Bathe in imbiza.

You can't get it up? Imbiza for you.

It's been up for more than four hours after taking the little blue pill? Guess what? Imbiza will sort it out.

You can't help being a racist? Take two tablespoons of imbiza, sit down and shut the fuck up.

You can't help being a homophobe? A big, fat imbiza enema for you, buddy.

Misogyny is your thing? Teabag your nuts in imbiza of boiling imbiza.

You want to lose weight? I recommend imbiza. It'll help you shed kilos by shitting out your internal organs. Sure, you'll die, but all the fat bitches at your funeral will be so jealous.

You want to gain weight? Yup, imbiza. It'll collapse your kidneys and you'll start retaining water. Dialysis shmialysis.

The woman of your dreams wants a circumcised man, but you're the kind of um'Zulu who ain't got time for that? Imbiza will shrink that skin right back.

You want your hair to be smooth, silky and voluminous? Wash it in imbiza.

You're tired of hair and want to go bald? Wash your head in imbiza.

You're dead from imbiza poisoning? Don't panic. Imbiza yase-Kwezi will bring you back to life.[15]

(NB: If your secret crush is currently dating a man who uses imbiza, or she just broke up with someone who is a user, move along. Los daai goeters.)

---

15 iKwezi is a train station in Soweto where a big traditional medicine market is situated.

If you didn't grow up in a mbiza-obsessed community, your Zulu credentials are suspect. Even if your immediate family is or was too good for imbiza, you should have relatives who swear by it. And by 'swear', I mean, 'Uyanya, wena mfana. Imbiza wu go-guarantee (You know nothing, foolish boy).'

Here are a few people who are clearly on a serious mbiza regimen – ubaba ka Duduzane, stepmom sika Duduzane, ubhuti ka Duduzane, cousin ka Duduzane, Duduzane.

People who are definitely not on imbiza – me. I am *such* a bad um'Zulu.

Warning: After even the smallest dose of imbiza, it is not advisable that you operate heavy machinery. In fact, don't do anything. Just get into the foetal position, suck your thumb and weep. Weep long and hard.

Disclaimer: I am not a medical doctor, a nurse, an orderly, or even a hospital receptionist. Nor am I a traditional healer or a pharmacist. I am not even a drug dealer. If you take medical advice from me then immediately drop dead, it's entirely your own fault.

ISUKILE

Isukile is related to suka (move) and susa (remove). As such, the word means 'it has moved' or 'it is off'.

So, what has moved or is off? Nothing. Everything. In this context, isukile is akin to the Afrikaans 'hier kom kak' (a shit-storm is brewing).

When the wife goes shopping. Isukile.

When the EFF rises on a point of order. Isukile.

When the blue lights flash behind you. Isukile.

When 'Omunye phez' komunye' comes on. Isukile.

When the girlfriend says she'll be ready in five minutes. Isukile.

When a certain former president has to read this number: 156 852 200.23. Isukile.

When the husband goes out for 'just one drink with the guys'. Isukile.

When your toddler starts sniffling and tears well up in his eyes. Isukile.

When Gert from Finance hears 'dzuuuum, dzum, dzum, dzum, dzuum, dzuuuum, nkalakatha'. Isukile.

When a slay queen sees a Nigerian buy a bottle of champagne. Isukile.

When the wife starts with 'you know how much I love you ...'. Isukile.

When Grace Mugabe pulls out an electric cord. Isukile.

When you're summoned to HR the morning after the Christmas party. Isukile.

When you take the car to the mechanic. Isukile.

When it's time to go through your teenager's school report. Isukile.

When the girlfriend says, 'We need to talk.' Isukile.

When ratings agencies come to town. Isukile.

When Steve Komphela opens his mouth. Isukile.

When Mmusi Maimane puts on the black accent. Isukile.

When you hear KE DIZEMBA, BOSS![16] Isukile.

When you live in South Africa. Isukile.

---

16 This is a universally known expression that signals the beginning of December and all its shenanigans.

LINDA

Linda is a popular Nguni name. It's used by both genders, but when a girl or woman is called Linda, we never know whether she is a Nguni or a European Linda.

Speaking of European Lindas, the first time I encountered a white Linda I honestly thought her parents had given her a Nguni name, like the Thandis and Tandis I know. Then I encountered a Lynda and thought she'd also been given a Nguni name, but her parents just wanted to give it a twist that would ensure that those who read it immediately knew she was white. That's important for things like renting property.

It was a real shock to discover that Linda is also a completely stand-alone European name. I still don't know what it means, though. Does it have a meaning?

Anyway, I've decided that all white South African Lindas and Lyndas are really using the Nguni Linda.

In isiZulu, a Nguni language, Linda means to wait or be patient. This means Linda and Patience are the same name. Since black names are so difficult to say, we should rename all white Lindas 'Patience' to make it easy for their friends, family and even themselves to say.

White Linda, you'll seriously make everyone's life so much easier by calling yourself Patience. You can still use Linda when you're with black people, but not with whites. You don't want your loved ones to hurt themselves trying to say your complicated Bantu name, do you? Exactly.

Don't fight me on this. It's worked for black people for hundreds of years. You'll see, it will do wonders for you.

Black Lindas can remain Linda.

ZAMA

Zama is to attempt or try. It is also the rubbish name of a rubbish girl who broke my heart twenty years ago. I had just moved into my own place in Sunninghill and had bought Nando's for dinner, and she'd slept over.

Yes, yes, good times. But that's not the point. I had some Nando's left over and was planning to eat it the next day, after work. When I returned, she had eaten it. I was devastated – I couldn't touch her ever again.

I recently saw her walking with her husband and kids, and I threw up in my mouth a little. I am not over her betrayal. Sies.

Zama is an important word and concept. Uyazama means 'he or she is not too bad' or 'you are not too bad'. In its innocent form, it means 'he or she is trying' or 'you are trying'. While it could be used in an encouraging manner, it can also be used to belittle someone's efforts. You could be the smartest person in the world, but your achievements could be reduced to 'hmm, uyazama'.

Is Nomzamo Mbatha the hottest celebrity woman in South Africa? Hmm, uyazama.

Is Wayde van Niekerk an amazing athlete? Hmm, uyazama.

Is Cyril Ramaphosa an extremely rich man? Hmm, uyazama shem.

Is Chief Justice Mogoeng Mogoeng an honourable man? Hmm, uyazama-nyana.[17]

Is Caster Semenya an inspiration? Woo, uyazama 'yaz.

Is Kagiso Rabada amazing? Uyazama for a cricket player.

Is Oscar Mdlongwa a legend? Uyazama.

---

17 See '-Nyana', p. 160.

Zama as a name can also refer to a clan name and mean 'of the' – for instance, Zama Ntungwa is 'of the Ntungwas'.

KONJE

Konje relates to memory and remembering. The closest thing in English is 'by the way', but konje has other uses, too. For example, one might ask, 'Konje, are any of Steve Hofmeyr's childrenseseses mixed-race?' because you know how these racist types actually love them some chocolate.

Konje can also mean 'oh, yes, I remember'. One day you walk past a woman, her husband and their two kids, and you let out a loud 'nx'. Your friend asks what's wrong, and you remind him: that woman is Zama, who once ate your last piece of Nando's. In that case, the friend will respond by saying, 'Koooooonje. Sathane. Nx!'

Here are more examples of how to use konje.

You walk from one room to another, then stop and ask, 'Konje, why am I in here? Konje, what was I looking for again?'

You're crying because Gogo Winnie Mandela has passed away, but you try playing it down by saying it's the first time you've cried. Your wife reminds you that you also shed a tear when you heard that Gundi and Mazwi[18] had gone off air so you respond, 'Konje, you're the devil's butt crack.' In this instance, konje means 'you have just reminded me'.

You've just smoked weed. 'Konje, what's my name? Why are we here? Konje, who created God?'

---

18 *Gundi no Mazwi* was a hilarious SABC1 kiddies' TV show featuring puppets. Completely unsuitable for kids, it was so hilarious that some of us watched it deep into our twenties.

You're out to lunch with your ex, thinking about patching things up, but he chews loudly and talks while chewing. *Kooooooooooonje.*

You watch a movie with your wife for the first time in a while and she keeps asking you what's going on, even though you're also seeing the movie for the first time: 'Konje this is why we don't go to the movies.'

You come home and one of the kids has ripped a hole in the couch: 'Konje this is why we can't have nice things.'

WENA NA

One of the reasons I keep starting different companies is because I don't like dreading Mondays. I don't like having a miserable boss, one who is simply waiting to take his or her misery out on me.

Somewhere, a Zulu person has just read this sentence and said, 'Wena na.'

It means 'I am not impressed'. It also means, 'I don't believe you. There is no way you can be that happy. There is no way things can be going that well. It's just not how life works.'

When Trevor Noah said he was going to host *The Daily Show*, a Zulu person said, 'Wena na.'

When Nelson Mandela said he was going to be the first black president of South Africa, a Zulu member of the PAC said, 'Wena na.'

When Wayde van Niekerk said he was going to be world champion, a Zulu coloured (yes, you know those ones – very dark, but still racist) said, 'Wena na, ma se kind.'

When Caster Semenya said she was a girl, a Zulu girl said, 'Wena na.' That Zulu girl was wrong to have said that.

When Chief Justice Mogoeng Mogoeng said Zuma must pay back the money, Msholozi said, 'Wena na.'

When Julius Malema said he'd stop being corrupt and make us forget about what he did in Polokwane, a Zulu person said, 'Wena na.'

When Helen Zille said white people brought us civilisation, a Zulu person said, 'Nina na.' (Nina is the plural of wena.)

When Mmusi Maimane put on a black accent, a Zulu person said, 'Wena na.'

When Jesus said he was going to turn water into wine, a Zulu Jew said, 'Wena na.'

When a young man went down on one knee, pulled out a ring and told a Zulu girl he wanted to spend the rest of his life with her, she said, 'Wena na.'

When you make the most amazing plans, uNkulunkulu (Zulu God) says, 'Wena na.'

Wena na is an all-purpose term to piss on everyone's party. The English equivalent is 'Really? You?', but this just doesn't have the same effect. We are big party poopers. We. Will. Poop. On. Your. Party.

Wena is 'you'. Na lets you know it's a question (a rhetorical one).

ABANGANI

Abangani means friends. Abangani are important. They are always there when we need them. Take this scenario, for instance.

The phone rings.

ME: Yo.

FRIEND: I am leaving Paulina. I'm done, man.

ME: Is it because of her name? You knew she was called Paulina when you asked her out. I told you she had an apartheid name.

FRIEND: No, man! I am not leaving because of her name, which, while unfortunate, is not a deal-breaker.

ME: Is it the smelly armpits, then?

FRIEND: What? My girlfriend doesn't have smelly armpits. WTF?

ME: Yeah, she does. That's why I never hug her.

FRIEND: Whatever. Anyway, I am leaving her because she called my olive oil fish oil.

ME: Noooooooooo! What a savage! I knew she wasn't right for you, but this is downright disgusting.

FRIEND: I am devastated, jo. Let's go drink.

ME: We have no choice but to drink.

Ah, abangani. If you don't have abangani you can be crazy with, you'll never lead a full life.

The singular is umngani.

DAKIWE

Dakiwe means to be drunk.

I am reminded of a funny heated argument that a group of drunk friends of mine once had. It went like this.

GUY 1: What is the point of you?

GUY 2: My point of view is …

GUY 1: No, the point of you! *You!*

GUY 2: Yes, my point of view is …

This went on for a few minutes, until another, slightly less dakiwe friend said, 'Hayi, futsek, man! Nidakiwe.'

133

Nidakiwe is you are drunk (plural). Singular is udakiwe. Udakiwe could be you are drunk or he or she is drunk, depending on the intonation.

IPHUNGA

Iphunga is a smell. It could be a good or a bad smell.

This word reminds me of the time I asked my wife to buy me roll-on and she bought me Brut. I think it was sometime in 2016. I ended up smelling like 1993 and like Smal Street and Club Arena. My smell was of S-curl and kwaito, Mashwabana and silk shirts.

I smelled like freedom was coming tomorrow. Like Mandela was alive and Madiba magic was going to save us.

ISIKHUMBA

Isikhumba is 'hide' and 'skin'. Both animals and people have isikhumba.

This word reminds me of a time when I was driving to a meeting with a fellow m'Zulu. He spotted a sign that read 'Nguni hides' and screamed, 'Never! Nguni never hides. Hide for what?'

In South Africa, isikhumba is such an important thing. For a long time, the colour of your isikhumba determined your station in life. It determined how you were viewed and treated. The colour of your isikhumba used to be the be-all and end-all. Sad, really.

This obsession with the colour of isikhumba led to the tragedy that is skin-lightening creams. What a bunch of madness. The legacy of skin-lightening creams has not disappeared, though. You still have people who have pink faces, while the rest of their bodies are brown. They look like strawberry-tipped chocolate ice lollies.

I am not judging; just observing.

I love my isikhumba, and I hope you love yours, too.

UKUPHINGA

Ukuphinga is adultery. I used to think God was against the idea of growing up, hence the disdain for adultery. Then, my English improved. Argh. It turns out he is all for growing up; it's ukuphinga he doesn't like.

UMYENI

Umyeni is a husband.

This word reminds me of an interesting conversation that took place between former colleagues of mine.

COLLEAGUE 1 (after getting off the phone): Husbandry sucks.

COLLEAGUE 2: What the hell do you know about husbandry?

COLLEAGUE 1: Dude, I've been a husband longer than you.

COLLEAGUE 2 (laughing): That is not husbandry, moron.

COLLEAGUE 3: I guess you've never seen his wife.

NGAZIFAKA

Ngazifaka is related to faka, which is to insert or put in.

Ngazifaka is an expression of regret, similar to that moment when you think, *What the hell have I got myself into?* For instance, you agree to take part in a week-long workshop, knowing you'll regret it the moment it starts; as expected, the regret kicks in, right on time.

Even as you were driving to the venue, all that was running through your mind was, *Ngazifaka. A week-long workshop in Jan always lasts a month.*

This feeling is not new to me, nor to most of us. We all get ourselves into these situations and then have no one to blame but ourselves.

The Tinder crowd knows all about ngazifaka. It's their mating call.

Our mate Brian Molefe should now be called Brain 'Ngazifaka' Molefe.

I don't know if Allister Coetzee speaks an African language, but I bet he knows ngazifaka very well. It must have been vuurwarm in the belly of the Bok. Or was he in its poephol?

If you took up a job in Cape Town in the past few years, you're screaming, 'Ngazifaka, yoh!' That water situation is no joke.

If you've ever taken a Gupta tender, we know what you're feeling right now.

If you join one of those hectic aerobic exercise classes and immediately think ngazifaka, don't be embarrassed to leave. You don't owe anyone stamina, baba.

That said, thinking ngazifaka doesn't necessarily mean you should quit straight away. I've got some really awesome results from situations I initially regretted.

NB: Faka, the root word, is not where the word 'fuck' comes from, even though ngazifaka does kind of mean 'I've fucked myself' and you could say ngazi fuck-a.

FI

Fi is an expression you use when you want to convey that something is really, really dead. It's related to fa, the Zulu word for die. Here is an example of how it works.

PERSON 1: uNjabulo ufile (Njabulo is dead).

PERSON 2: Fi (Really dead)?

PERSON 1: Fi, fi, fi (Really, really dead).

PERSON 2: Fi, fi, fi, fi (Really, really, really dead)?

PERSON 1: Fi, fi, fi, fi, fi (Like, dead, dead, dead, dead).

PERSON 2: Fi, fi, fi, fi, fi, fi (For real)?

PERSON 1: Fi (Yup)!

PERSON 2: Nx (What a loser / I don't believe you / He owes me money) …

LAHLILE

Lahlile is related to the word lahla, which means to throw away, to lose, to break up with or to be sexually available, as in open to someone's advances.

Lahlile means you're reckless, naive, gullible, unguarded, fair game, unprepared, or even stupid. In essence, you're like a thing that has been thrown away. You're up for the taking. South Africa is not the kind of place you want to be ulahlile.

With this word, we'll play a little game: I'll start a sentence and you finish it by adding 'lahlile' in your head, or even out loud. I think this will help internalise the word so you'll be vigilant as you go about your business, living your best life. Here we go:

B.A. Baracus pities you because you're a fool and u …

Guys pay thousands of rands for women's weaves because ba …

The Dutch East India Company found us si …

If you believe he loves you just because he says so, u …

If you support Orlando Pirates, u …

AKA's manager got slapped by a one-armed man because u …

When getting married, women take men's surnames because ba …

Trap (the music style) is popular because youngsters ba …

If we were to get invaded by another country, they'd find us si …

If you have unprotected sex, u …

Mugabe was president for such a long time because ama-Zimbabwean a …

If you don't take the listeria warnings seriously, u …

Zuma believed Nkosazana would become president because he figured iANC i …

DA made Mmusi its leader, yet doesn't have meaningful policies, because they think si …

Thabo Mbeki got recalled because ube …

The ANC lost the Johannesburg, Tshwane and Nelson Mandela metros because ba …

The ANC might lose the 2019 national elections because ba …

If you let a waiter walk away with your card, u …

If you let a stranger help you at the ATM, u …

If you leave your drink unattended at the bar, u …

u = you/he/she is

ba = they are

si = we are/we were

be ka = he/she was

a = they are

MOYIZELA

Moyizela is to smile. Even saying the word out loud encourages you to smile. Try it.

Moyizela makes me think of two teenagers smiling sheepishly at each other across the room in church. Their respective mothers think they're smiling because the preacher's words have filled their hearts with the wonder that is Jesus' love. But the truth is, they're smiling because they've let the devil camp out in their pants. It's a thing of beauty.

Ukumoyizela (to moyizela) can be a weapon of mass destruction. It breaks down walls, invades hearts and conquers souls.

That said, it's useless on a pissed-off Zulu mother. You've screwed up (again), she's pissed off (again), so you smile, hoping it will melt her heart, but she just hits you with a cynical 'uya sineka' and that stupid smile is quickly wiped off your stupid face.

Sineka means grin and is related to izinsini (gums). So, ukusineka (to sineka) means to expose your gums and no one likes being accused of exposing their gums like an idiot.

CATHAMA

Cathama is to walk softly or sneak.

The name of the music genre isicathamiya is derived from cathama. Isicathamiya is a capella Zulu music. The brightest light in this genre is the multiple Grammy Award-winning group Ladysmith Black Mambazo, even though there's a massive movement beyond Black Mambazo.

In the context of isicathamiya, the verb ukucathama refers to the genre's so-called soft-touch dance and singing styles.

Legend has it that isicathamiya was created by migrant workers who performed Zulu music and dance in their employers' back yards and back rooms while preparing for weekend competitions. However, because of apartheid laws and their asshole employers who forbade any kind of normal human behaviour, they had to sneak around and ensure they didn't get caught. It didn't help that traditional Zulu dance is so robust: it makes a noise and cracks cement floors.

To deal with this need to cathama around, they got rid of their musical instruments and developed the soft-touch singing and dance styles. This style of music and dance came to be known as isicathamiya – the sneak-around music.

It spread like wildfire, and went on to mesmerise local and international audiences.

GIJIMA

Gijima is to run. Not necessarily 'run towards a dodgy tender', like that one infamous IT company we know.

What I don't like is when a person is quite a distance ahead of me but courteously holds the door open for me after he or she has walked through. WTF? Now I must run because if I continue walking at my desired pace I'm an unappreciative prick? Great, now I am running, even though I am not rushing anywhere. 'Tsek, nice person, for making me gijima.

I know people who'd just let you stand there like an idiot. I admire them.

XHAWULA

Xhawula is to shake hands.

Handshakes mean so much. I didn't know why white men squeezed your hand so hard until I was told that a firm handshake means you're a solid man, especially in business. Whatever; you're hurting my hand.

Then you have the intricate dude handshakes. Some of them look so cool. But a man with long fingernails shouldn't xhawula with intricate dude handshakes. It can be dangerous. Take it easy there, Freddy Krueger.

(BTW, I used to think Freddy Krueger was Freddy Kruger, an Afrikaner. Hey, it was during apartheid; all the boogeymen were Afrikaans.)

XAKEKA

Xakeka is to be confused or to be in a bind.

In a country with cultures and languages as diverse as ours, it's easy to xakeka. For instance, whenever my white friends use the word Aussie in a text, I think they're talking about the lady who looks after their kids.

WHITE PERSON: I hate that Aussie.

ME: Heh? What did aussie do? Did she seduce your man?

The actual words people some use for nannies and helpers are ousie, sisi, or aunty.

UMSEBENZI

Umsebenzi is 'to work' or 'worker', depending on the intonation.

However, umsebenzi is also a colloquial term for a traditional ceremony. Here is a wonderful example of the different ways in which it can be used.

Vegetarian umsebenzi to colleague: Come through to the house tomorrow. We have umsebenzi.

Carnivore umsebenzi: You're gonna slaughter a pumpkin?

After that brief pear-shaped exchange, everyone knew it was time leave umsebenzi and start their weekend.

UMLINGO

Umlingo is magic.

I've always wanted to go to an umlingo show, but I suspect it would just upset me because I'd want to know how they pull off all the tricks. This is the same reason why I'd never be part of these 'miracle' churches.

KHOHLWA

Khohlwa is to forget. The following words are related to it:

Khohliwe is to be forgotten.

Khohlisa is to deceive.

Khohlisiwe is to be deceived.

Khohliseka is to be naïve.

Khohlakele is to be deceitful, corrupt or evil.

Inkohlakalo is deceit, corruption or evil.

Ikholwa is a believer (a Christian).

Kholiwe is to have believed.

What a massive difference an h can make!

You see, the Zulu ancestors were honest Christians (ama-

142

kholwa) until a Mosotho stranger, we'll call him Mosebenzi Magashule-Lekota, deceived them. As this weird man in a blanket in summer told lie after lie, trying to make them forget their truth, a collective 'ha' was heard across the lands of all the Nguni peoples. Because 'ha' is the phonetic of 'h', the Council for Giving isiZulu Names and Words to Foreign (Sotho) Words, Concepts and General Foreign Shit (CFGiZNAWTFWCAGFS) added 'h' to the 'kholwa' set of words and the 'khohlwa' set was born.

Seriously, this is all true. You must kholwa me.

(BTW, what kind of nonsense name is Mosebenzi? The isiZulu word is umsebenzi or umusebenzi. The 'mo' is a seSotho thing, so the name Mosebenzi is some sort of Zulu–Sotho fanakalo.[19] I tell you, it's not a name. It's a lie, a corruption. This man must tell us his real name. He and Malusi must stop khohlisa-ing us because we're not gon' be all right until they come clean.

NB: Pronounced correctly, 'hl' sounds like the sizzle and crackle of frying steak.

ULAYEKILE

We see a lot of talk about karma on the Internet. In isiZulu, we just say ulayekile. Ulayekile means 'it serves you right'.

The word is related to laya, which means to guide or advise. So ukuluyeka is to learn the hard way, which is good for you, which is why it serves you right. If ulayekile, life has taught

---

19 If Mosebenzi is not a Mosotho, I declare him a honorary one. You can keep him. Asimufuni.

you a lesson. We are not mocking you; we are, in fact, happy for you.

Are you a loud-mouthed, attention-seeking minister who couldn't stop tweeting, but have now been demoted to your party's Head of Elections? Some would say ulayekile.

Did you get into bed with a party that's your ideological opposite to secure certain metros, but now that party is turning on you and wanting to hand those metros back to a party they are ideologically closer to? Nilayekile (serves you (plural) right).

Did you tell Juju your secrets and Juju told the world? Ulayekile.

Did you drive inside the yellow line while the 'idiots' sat stuck in traffic, but are now being hauled off to a holding cell because you were driving under the influence? Ulayekile.

Did you steal your colleague's lunch from the fridge and are now dying because of the poison his wife had put in his food? Ulayekile.

Did you buy a sex doll to show your girlfriend that you could easily replace her, but your penis got electrocuted? Ulayekile.

Did you buy a dildo to let your man know you're not satisfied, but now your kid and his friends are playing with it at the neighbour's? Ulayekile.

Did you think you're better than other people because you afford to shop at Woolies, but now you've got frostbite? Ulayekile.

At a red light, did you get out of your car to go swear at another driver, but got back to your car to find the door locked? Ulayekile.

In a taxi on your way to work, did you text a friend about how ugly a fellow commuter's kid is, and then the kid threw upon you? Ulayekile.

Did you call a fellow motorist a fucking bitch as you were stealing her parking, and she turned out to be the interviewer in your job interview? Ulayekile.

Melusi, did you just make fun of other people's misfortune? Uzolayeka.

Uzolayeka means you will get what you deserve or learn your lesson.

INYONGO

No, not Lupita Nyong'o, even though we'd give her an honorary Zuluship if she wanted it. In fact, we hereby officially adopt her as um'Zulu.

Inyongo is bile and gallbladder. Inyongo also means nonsense, like Cyril's (not-so-) new Cabinet.

But most importantly, inyongo is a mythical ailment that can cause:

Nausea

Lethargy

Erectile dysfunction

Premature ejaculation

Diarrhoea

Bad moods

Halitosis

Body odour

Excessive gas

Skin conditions

Body pains
Puffy eyes
Red eyes
Stupidity
State capture
And so much more.

Inyongo can be cured with imbiza (taken orally), ukucha-tha (an enema), ukuphalaza (induced vomiting) and laxatives. In children, whose inyongo is often attributed to a diet heavy on sweets, the preferred methods are ukuchatha and laxatives. But you need to catch the kids before you can administer any sort of treatment.

Interestingly, once you leave your family home and strike out on your own, it is really only your fault if you ever suffer from inyongo again. A lot of people choose to not suffer from inyongo and attribute their symptoms to other, more univer-sally recognised, ailments, like alcoholism.

My inyongo definitely got permanently cured once I was old enough to tell my grandmother, 'Hell, no. Nothing is going up my butt.'

BROKEN TELEPHONE

Let's deal with a bunch of words and expressions relating to the concept of a broken telephone. There is no specific phrase for broken telephone in isiZulu. The closest I can think of is 'ukuphambana kwezinkomishi' – the mixing up of cups – but I could be wrong.

Broken telephone would be directly translated thus: ucingo (a telephone or wire) oluphukile (that is broken).

While the word for telephone is ucingo, television is mabona kude (see far). Shouldn't telephone be makhuluma kude (talk from afar), or malalela kude (listen from afar), or maxoxela kude (chat from afar)?

No, ucingo works better. Plus, malalela kude could also mean 'one who prefers to sleep far away'. I have married friends who fit this description.

The Council for Giving isiZulu Names and Words to Foreign Words and General Foreign Shit (CFGiZNAWTFWAGFS) is full of wise elders, so they always make great decisions. Like when they named the cellphone makhala ekhukhwini. I think not. Makhala ekhukhwini is 'that which rings in the pocket'. Khala is both ring and cry. Makhala is a thing or person that rings or cries a lot.

There are several glaring issues with this name, the first being that most dresses and skirts don't have pockets. Maybe the CFGiZNAWTFWAGFS should be more representative.

But back to makhala ekhukhwini. It's a good thing the people who confused the airline Kulula and khulula were not involved in deciding on a name for the cellphone, because makhala ekukwini (without the h) would be something else altogether.[20]

Makhala is also both nose and noses. As such, umakhala could be a crybaby (Brian Ngazifaka Molefe) or someone with a big nose. The two versions are pronounced slightly differently.

Shoo, so much possibility for a broken telephone. And that's not even the half of it.

---

20 Makhala ekukwini is the expression for someone who cries during sex. Ekukwini = inside the koekie.

IMILENZE

Imilenze is legs.

Here is a good example for how to use it. Two Zulu guys are hanging out having a beer when an Afrikaner man in shorts walks by. The one guy turns to his friend and says, 'Yoh, that's imilenze.'

His friend responds, 'Ya, white people have really big legs. It's from all that Groot Trekking.'

NQUNU

Nqunu means to be naked. When explaining nqunu, I can't help thinking about Adam and Eve.

So, Adam and Eve are hanging out in the garden of Ennerdale (yes, they are coloured), naked. No boner on Adam. Fine. I'm six years old when I first hear this story and I haven't grasped the full reach of the effects of the female form on the male phallus.

But when I get older, I think, *No, man.* So, this gazi and his stukkie are in the garden of Eden, nqunu, minding their own business, fearing God, when this snake arrives. He encourages Eve to eat an apple from the tree of the knowledge of evil and good, even though God has strictly forbidden it. It might make them cleverer, but they will also lose their wonderful life in the garden.

They don't want to lose everything. Who does?

But guess what? They fall for it. Over an apple. Not a mango. Or peach. Or banana. Or strawberry. Or granadilla.

Not even a Savanna.

I'm telling you, the snake was the excuse they needed to

get it on. That makes much more sense to me than throwing paradise away for an apple.

INTSANGU

Intsangu is dagga, ganja, marijuana, weed, or zol.

When I heard talk of intsangu being legalised, I was so confused. For as long as I've been alive, I've been surrounded by people who smoke with impunity. Not because they don't respect the law, but because the law has never been part of the discussion when it comes to zol.

It grows. It gets smoked. Finish and klaar.

I am reminded of a dear friend of mine, who said, 'Intsangu is a gateway drug, if you smoke it at Gateway.' He then proceeded to light up in the parking lot of said shopping mall.

I don't smoke, though. Used to, but I realised I make enough terrible decisions anyhow; I don't need the extra help.

UDOTI

Udoti is rubbish.

Sometimes my mind is full of doti and leads me astray. For instance, a few years back, I became aware of a mini-furore about some white woman who went around the country giving poor black people cake. I thought, *Now this is the spirit of reconciliation Madiba and that crazy old bishop were talking about. Where we used to have the Immorality Act, now we have a cute white girl satisfying the people's koekie needs.*

Then I realised she was giving them *cake* cake. And I thought,

WTF? What kind of white she-devil would poison my people with gluten? She could only be the daughter of Wouter Basson.

If that's not udoti thinking, I don't know what is.

VIKA

Vika means to ward off, shield, or evade.

When someone attempts to attack you, you vika. To protect is vikela.

Colloquially, ivika is the tobacco you mix with dagga to cushion you from the potency of the dagga. It vikelas you from the dagga so the dagga doesn't completely obliterate you.

Keeping with the colloquial use of vika, there are other things that can be described as vika instruments.

Toothpaste is ivika.

Deodorant is ivika.

Make-up is ivika.

Dash is ivika.

If you're a complete rubbish but are also religious, religion is your ivika.

If you're gay but are in a heterosexual relationship because of societal norms, your hetero partner is ivika.

If you're racist but have a black friend you yank out whenever it's convenient, your black 'friend' is your ivika.

If you spend all your time at work because your home life is miserable, your job is ivika.

If you drink just to cope, booze has become your ivika.

We all have our little vikas to vikela us as we navigate our way through life and its infinite twists and turns. If you're someone's vika, may you be the best vika in the world.

IBHOLA LOMBHOXO

Ibhola lombhoxo is rugby.

The Council for Giving isiZulu Words to Foreign Words, Concepts and General Foreign Shit (CFGiZWTFWCAGFS) could have Zulufied it and called it Lagbi. While that would have been good enough, it would not have let the world know how we feel about this sport.

The word mbhoxo sounds terrible; on top of that, it's isiXhosa. That's how much we couldn't be bothered. We could have called it ibhola lamaXhosa. Or ibhola lamabhunu. But instead, we went for 'shit soccer', in isiXhosa. Just kidding. It doesn't mean shit soccer.

Mbhoxo actually means oval. I suspect it comes from how oval things work. Think about how a rugby ball bounces. The ends bounce – mbho. The sides fall flat on their stupid faces, with a loud 'xo'. Nguni languages and onomatopoeia: same WhatsApp group. We obviously don't like oval things. Otherwise oval would have a better word.

That's why there is no rugby team called AmaZulu or Lamontville Golden Arrows. If the CFGiZWTFWCAOFS had called rugby lagbi or something other than ibhola lombhoxo (oval ball), things would be very different.

Ibhola lombhoxo sounds like a sport one shouldn't be caught dead playing. If you ask a kid wom'Zulu which sport she'd rather play – ibhola or ibhola lombhoxo – we all know the answer would be, 'Fokkof, lwabish (rubbish).'

To be honest, we have not done a great job of giving the

world's various ball sporting codes their own proper isiZulu names, so I've gone ahead and done so:

Tennis – ibhola loku memeza. Scream ball.

Hockey – ibhola lobu hlungu. Pain ball.

Volleyball – ibhola le arthritis.

Squash – ibhola le heart attack.

Golf – ibhola lezi dakwa ne corruption. Drunkard-and-corruption ball.

Badminton – ibhola lama simba. Waste of time ball.

Netball – ibhola le tswape. Wedgie ball.

Basketball – ibhola lama nigga. Figure it out for yourself.

Baseball – ibhola lama steroid. Steroid ball.

Cricket – ibhola loku robha. Cheating ball.

Cricket – ibhola lobu vila. Lazy ball.

Polo – ibhola loku zenza ngcono. Snob ball.

Water polo – ibhola loku zenza ngcono emanzini. Snob ball in water.

INJA

Inja is dog.

Black South Africans' love–hate relationship with dogs is well documented. This rocky relationship is reflected in how the word inja is used in relation to people. The meaning it carries depends on who is calling you a dog, and why.

If it's one of the neighbourhood old ladies, it's always a bad thing. She hates you even though you probably don't recall why. She may have Alzheimer's and remember nothing else, but she knows that uyi (you are) inja. Maybe you broke one of her windows while playing soccer in the 1980s, or you walked on her freshly polished stoep with your muddy North Stars, or you broke up with her granddaughter Thandi after she fell pregnant with another guy's baby, or you remind her of her own cheating husband who left her with four kids forty years ago. Who knows.

But to her, you are inja.

I am sorry, gogo ka Thandi, okay? We need to get past this before you die and go on to tell my ancestors lies about me. I'll gladly fight you if that's what you want. And don't think I'll let you win just because you're so old you could have given Madiba his first hickey.[21]

But back to inja.

If you're a man and a lover calls you inja, you've screwed up badly in the past, you are screwing up in the present, you're a fucking idiot, you're a fucking liar, you screwed someone who isn't her, and/or you're screwed.

But if you haven't wronged your lover and you are being called inja or inja yami, especially when she answers your calls, she's seeing someone else and she's playing both of you. In this instance, inja means buddy or homie, while inja yami means my buddy or my homie.

If you're a woman and your lover calls you inja or inja yami, especially when he answers your calls, he's seeing someone else and he's playing both of you.

Outside of romantic relationships, it's very easy to work out why you're being called inja and whether it's meant in a positive or a negative way.

---

21 It is never okay to fight with grannies. Even if they started it. Just walk away, man.

Are you awesome? Then uyinja.

Do you suck? Then uyinja.

Okay, maybe it's not that clear. Let's try to clarify it with more examples.

You score a goal and your teammate says, 'Sho, nja,' but the goalie says, 'Nja.' Your teammate means you're awesome, but the goalie means you suck.

You walk into the house after a late night out and your brother says, 'Ya, nja.' Your wife also says, 'Ya, nja.' Which is 'suck', which is 'awesome'? You should be able to work this one out for yourself.

Someone asks about you and your friend says, 'Ya, I know him, inja.' Someone asks about you and your ex says, 'Ya, I know her, inja nje.' Which is 'suck', which is 'awesome'? Same as above.

Your sister asks your wife, 'Iphi le nja yakho (Where is that dog of yours)?' Your wife responds, 'Who knows?' Your wife asks your sister, 'Iphi le nja yakini (Where is that dog you're related to)?' Your sister will either drop-kick or roundhouse-kick her.

Then there's inja ye game (I don't even know how to translate this), inja embi (bad dog or ugly dog), inja ka Sathane (the devil's dog), inja ewisa ama dustbin (dog that knocks over dustbins), inja engana mnikazi (ownerless dog), inja engakhuzeki (stubborn dog), and more. We also make them up as we go along. These can all mean that you are awesome. Or a complete piece of shit.

Except inja ye game. That always means awesome. But you could also be awesome at being a complete shit.

You can replace 'game' with any other word to signify the

thing someone is amazing at, for instance inja ye Twitter, inja ye corruption. We could go on and on, but as you can see, it's all very clear. Sho, zinja.

On a sombre note, inja is at the centre of toxic masculinity. Men have done, and continue to do, terrible and dumb things just to prove we are izinja. Just visit jails, hospitals, mortuaries and cemeteries – they are full of izinja. Hospitals, mortuaries and cemeteries are also full of people put there by izinja. We've got to do better.

AYIKHO LENKUKHU, AWACHITHWE LAMANZI

There's this thing where silly people spitefully joke about black people's love for chicken. Well, vele![22] We love chicken. We love other things too, but ya, we love chicken. It's yummy, affordable, readily available and small enough to slaughter without much fuss.

You can also keep chickens as pets. Then eat them. What amazing things are pets that one can also eat. 'Oh, chicken, you're my son's best friend in the whole wide world. But now I'm going to behead you, put your carcass in a dish of scalding water, pluck you, season you, then stick you in the oven. It's gonna be a party. Melusi's fortieth birthday party.'

Kidding – my family buys chickens pre-murdered now. We no longer eat our children's friends.

This little bit of gruesomeness brings me to the following isiZulu expression. It's what you say when you're done with

---

22 Vele is an affirmation and an act of defiance. See p. 159.

bekezeling (waiting or enduring[X]). The expression is, 'Ayikho lenkukhu, awachithwe lamanzi (There is no chicken, let's spill this water).'

The expression relates to someone who is trying to prepare a chicken dish, but fails. You've sent someone to buy, catch, or slaughter a live chicken and you have the scalding water in the dish, ready for the plucking. You wait and wait and wait. Maybe you've even had to reheat the water a couple of times.

Eventually, you realise that, for whatever reason, there will be no chicken for your fortieth birthday. Maybe the money went to booze (we all know that uncle), or the chicken ran away or died of Newcastle (a fowl disease). Whatever. At some point you have to accept that the chicken will not materialise, so you throw out the water and move on with your life.

In friendship, business, politics, marriage, or any other relationship, it often happens that the proverbial chicken never materialises. Try as you might to be patient with it, or hope that it'll see the light and change, at some point you have to admit to yourself that ayikho lenkukhu, awachithwe lamanzi.

Of course you're sad, because you really wanted chicken. But guess what? Now you can go have some wagyu.

Disclaimer: No vegetarians, vegans or animal rights activists were intentionally offended when I wrote this piece. Even the really sensitive ones. I swear.

PS: AbeZulu also love watermelon (ihabhu), which is delicious and nutritious. Since it's ninety-two per cent water, Capetonians should really also get into it.

IDLOZI

Idlozi is an ancestor.

Amadlozi is the plural of idlozi. Amadlozi are those who came before us and who now guide us, protecting us from the spirit world. They can also be a pain in the ass. No, amadlozi are not ghosts or evil spirits. And no, you cannot dress your kid as idlozi to go trick or treating on Halloween.

Even though Christianity is now the dominant religion in South Africa, amadlozi are still an important part of life for a significant portion of the Zulu population. I have questions about this aspect of (after)life:

Does everyone who passes on become idlozi? I certainly hope not.

How long does it take you to become idlozi after you've passed? Is it one moment you're doing the Vosho, the next the Vosho kills you, and boom! you're idlozi? Or is there a waiting period? I suggest a waiting period and proper vetting.

Is it possible to have idlozi with low self-esteem who thinks your dreams are too big? I know some people who'd be this kind of idlozi.

What if you were just plain stupid while roaming the earth? Do you immediately gain otherworldly wisdom, or do you become a stupid dlozi?

What if you worked really hard while on earth and just want to rest once you're on the other side? Do the other amadlozi give you dirty looks and talk behind your back until you feel so bad that you relent and then become one of those grumpy dlozis who complicate people's lives? You know those ones.

Do you have amadlozi who are overly enthusiastic, sticking their noses in other clans' matters? Does the spirit world ever hear, 'Hayi fokof, Macingwane, man. Jesus, ndoda. Fall back!'?

Has idlozi ever said, 'Hayi, futsek. Awachithwe lamanzi, ayikho lenkukhu'? One of yours probably has.

What if your descendants are Model C's and reach out to you in English? Do you just pretend you're not there?

What if your descendants are reaching out to you about really dumb shit? Do you care if they want a man with a car?

Is there a dlozi app that keeps amadlozi updated on what the kids on earth are yapping to them about? Is the app called iDlozi? Do you consult iDlozi when a spoilt brat is upset he doesn't have Netflix?

How often do amadlozi facepalm because people have become so entitled and keep wanting more?

Do amadlozi recognise their descendants through layers and layers of make-up, amashiya (eyebrows) on fleek and Brazilian weaves?

What if the dlozi who loves you the most became idlozi because he was killed by apartheid police, but now you're marrying an Afrikaner? Does idlozi turn on you, or are amadlozi not petty?

If you find this post disrespectful, take it up with amadlozi akini. Mine are fine with it. In fact, your ancestors reached out to my ancestors to get them to ask me to write this in the hope that you might see it and stop your shit. Sho, dlozi.

Dlozi is also a term of endearment and a playful way of saying someone is bloody old.

PS: With so many black people having abandoned the African ways in favour of 'more modern' approaches, some amadlozi are extremely lonely, including those who were abandoned hundreds of years ago. To tackle this problem, I have set up an initiative called Adopt-Idlozi.

For a nominal fee, Adopt-Idlozi gives white people access to amadlozi they can claim as their own. To mitigate the risk of dlozi abuse, I run a strict vetting process and assign people amadlozi suited specifically to them. If you get a nyaope dlozi, I surely picked up something about you that says you deserve that kind of dlozi in your life. Inbox me for banking details.

VELE

Vele is an affirmation and an act of defiance. It's equivalent to 'yeah, I said it, so what?', 'yeah, I am, so what?' or 'yeah, I did it, so what?' Only, it's more powerful.

By using vele, you own yourself, your actions and your decisions. You're saying you don't care what the world thinks. Or that, even if you do care, you're not giving people the satisfaction of knowing you do. You can also use it to disempower those who are trying to shame, belittle or corner you.

From here onwards, I'm writing VELE in capitals – not because it's an acronym, but because it has to be said with impact. Not shouted, just said without flinching or fear.

If you're wearing a weave and someone snarkily asks whether it's a weave, you don't sheepishly stutter, 'Yes.' You respond with, 'VELE!'

I've even seen a quick, sharp VELE shut down a homophobe.

If you're confronted about some piece of gossip you've been spreading, you don't backtrack. After all, you're already a gossip; you can't be a coward, too. Just say, 'VELE, you stole the land/ate the Gupta curry/play for Bafana Bafana.'

A good friend will try to defend you. A great friend will say VELE on your behalf if you're too slow on the trigger.

Sometimes, you shouldn't even let a fool finish his statement or question. Simply hit him with a sharp VELE jab on his loud mouth, as soon as he opens it. If the provocateur has an accomplice, it's always best to go this route: Robin may throw in a quick VELE in support of his Batman. Don't let them get theirs in before yours.

If you're really in the mood, you can even throw in an 'and?' after the VELE. But you've got to be prepared for whatever comes next.

Remember: no retreat. No surrender.

-NYANA

Yes, this is the -nyana of smallanyana skeletons.

This suffix is a diminutive – it denotes the smaller form of something. For instance, a boy is umfana, a small boy is umfanyana; a girl is intombazane, a little girl is intombazanyana; a mouth is umlomo, a small mouth is umlonyana; an animal is isilwane and a small animal is isilwanyana. In some ways, -nyana works like the Afrikaans diminutive -tjie.

This suffix can be applied to many words, but not to all.

Actually, I lie. Traditionally, there are many words it doesn't go with. But because language, like Zodwa,[23] belongs to the people, it has come to work the way people want it to. Where a bit of impuphu (powder) should be impushana, you'll now hear people say impuphunyana. IsiZulu purists hate this, but what are they gonna do?

The word is not strictly isiZulu; it exists in other languages, too, where it serves the same or a similar purpose. In Sesotho,

---

23 Zodwa is an infamous stripper who strips at public events.

you have ngwanyana (girl) and moshimanyana (boy). It doesn't stop there; these days, the suffix has transcended its roots and invaded everyday southern African speak. Even a bit of hummus can be hummus-nyana, while what happened in Zim is a coup-nyana.

It can also be used as a stand-alone word to downplay something:

GENEROUS FRIEND: Are you hungry?

TACTFUL FRIEND: Nyana.

Or another example:

NOSY FRIEND: How did the date go? Did you ... you know what?

BASHFUL FRIEND: Nyana.

NOSY FRIEND: What the hell does that mean?

BASHFUL FRIEND: Mind your own business.

In the above two instances, nyana could mean maybe, sort of, or a little.

Here's yet another example:

GIRL 1: I think your crush is gay.

GIRL 2: Nyana, neh?

GIRL 1: Not nyana. Gay, gay.

GIRL 2: Nyana, man!

In the above example, it means a little, a bit, or a hint of.

PS: In isiXhosa, nyana means son.

JIKA

No, not jika (pronounced jikh-ah) as in to use Jik, but jika as in to turn.

BTW, do they still make Jik? Just writing about it has brought that horrid smell back. All my wonderful childhood memories of my mother and warm feelings I have towards her have been tainted with that Jik smell. Because I'm spiteful, I hope your brain also has you smelling phantom Jik now.

My mother used to be a Jik junkie. Jik to soak the dishcloths. Jik to disinfect the kitchen. Jik to dilute the Jik. At times I suspected she used to do Jik shots. Thank God she kicked the habit.

Anyway, I digress. Back to jika – left at the robots, right at the taxi rank. Just don't let reading about directions make you think an isiZulu-speaking GPS would be a good idea. Unless you want your GPS mocking and swearing at you: 'Buka lesilima. Ngithe jika la, nja ndini. Awuna ngqondo. (Look at this idiot. I told you to turn here, bastard. You're the worst.[24])'

It's okay, let's stick with the white-lady GPS, even though we once got very lost because a friend of mine refused to take instructions from a white woman in Dizemba. He says he does enough of that during the rest of year.

Talking of Dizemba things: a derivative of jika is jikela – to turn on someone or something. No, not that kind of turn-on, Dizemba freaks. Turn on as in the tequila eventually turned on me and I spent the night throwing up in the loo.

Another is jikeleza – to beat around the bush or take the long way around, to wander, a.k.a. to meando.[25]

To jika also means to dance – not to bounce around, but to

---

24 Here is the literal translation: Buka = to look/look at, le = this, silima = idiot. Ngithe = I said, jike = turn, la = here, inja = dog, ndini = bloody (figurative). Awuna = you don't have, ngqondo = mind/sense. PS: Inja ndini will always jikela you.

25 During a Q&A session in Parliament in 2017, then-President Jacob Zuma used the word 'meandos' ('You come with meandos, I answer with meandos'). It is suspected he meant 'innuendos'.

go in hard. When you're dancing properly, you have to do a couple of turns. Therefore, jika. A person who loves to dance is majika. Jika, majika.

Now that's isiZulu for you …

IZINOMBOLO

Izinombolo means numbers. It is actually the English word 'numbers' that has been Zulufied. The singular is inombolo.

IsiZulu numbers are fine until you get to six. Then it all goes to shit. Six is isithupha, which is thumb. I just wonder, what if you don't have thumbs? Maybe they were blown off during the struggle. Now fellow abeZulu can't buy six-packs in isiZulu in front of you.

Seven is isikhombisa – the finger you point with. What if, like Msholozi, you point with your middle finger?

Eight is sishiyagalombili and nine is sishiyagalolunye. Sishiyagalombili means you leave two fingers. Sishiyagalolunye means you leave one finger. What fanakalo rubbish is that? Ten is ishumi. That's not even isiZulu. It's Shangaan. And you wonder why taxi drivers are so pissed off.

AMASHUMI AYISISHIYAGALOMBILI NESI-SHIYAGALOLUNYE

Amashumi ayisishiyagalombili nesishiyagalolunye sounds like it's something interesting, right? It's not. It's just eighty-nine.

IMPELA SONTO

Impela sonto is the weekend. The weekend means different things to different people. Some chill out; others wear themselves out. Some honour their god/s; others test theirs.

With that in mind, let's look at some isiZulu words and phrases with multiple uses and connotations:

Isibindi. Booze gives you isibindi, but also destroys it. That's because isibindi means both bravery and liver.

Amanzi. Amanzi is water, but amanzi amponjwana is 'water with horns'. Those horns give you isibindi and stab it at the same time. Yup, you guessed it – amanzi amponjwana is booze.

Shaya, shayela, shayisa. Shaya is to hit. Shayela is to drive. Shayisa is to get into a collision. Colloquially, shayisa also means to 'put out'.

Umuntu. Umuntu is a person. The word can also specifically mean a black African person.

Cansi. Ucansi is what you do. Icansi is where you do it. Ucansi is sex. Icansi is a straw mat. Amanzi amponjwana can give you isibindi to have ucansi with umuntu you're not supposed to have ucansi with.

Omusha. Umuntu omusha is a young person. Or a new person.

Hlobo. Ihlobo is a good time to visit isihlobo. Ihlobo is summer. Isihlobo is a relative. Legend has it that ihlobo and isihlobo are related because summer is, indeed, a good time to socialise.

Sika. Ubusika is when you cut ties with relatives and friends so you can hibernate. Ubusika is winter, sika is cut. Thank goodness ubusika does not last forever.

Ntatha and thatha. Thatha is to take. Dawn is ntathakusa (the time when the morning begins to take hold). Kusa relates to the morning, to awakening and becoming wiser. Staying out till intathakusa is how you get yourself into jail.

Sonto: Week, place of worship and Sunday. Oh, and a girl who once broke my heart.

On mpela sontos, we must remember to take it easy on isibindi, by going easy on amanzi amponjwana. Avoid random cansi, but make friends nomuntu omusha. Always make the most of ihlobo by seeing izihlobo. And please drink amanzi futhi ungashayisi.

MITHA

Zulufying gone wrong happens when the Council for Giving isiZulu Words and Names to Foreign Words, Concepts and General Foreign Shit (CFGiZNAWTFWCAGFS) decides they are busy with more important Zulu things, like helping Senzo Mchunu take his rightful place in the ANC top six. They failed at this

When this happens, unqualified abeZulu, like me, run rampant, giving their own names to all sorts of stuff. That is when you get words like Khongolose (African National Congress), itekisi (taxi) and stimela (steam train, although the word has come to refer to all trains).

Zulufying often leads to interesting results – like mitha, the Zulufied version of meet. However, mitha also means to fall pregnant. It's important to note that there is an actual, proper isiZulu word for meeting – ukuhlangana / umhlangano.

Now, with mitha, we have two such vastly different meanings you can imagine it's a recipe for ridiculousness. Like when two young women tell their grandmother they are going to a meeting:

Gogo: Niyaphi, bazukulu (Where are you going, grandchildren)?

Girl: Siyo mitha, gogo (We're going to a meeting).

Gogo: Hawu, kodwa ubufebe niyo buyeka nini? Noma nifuna imali yeqolo? 'Yaz nizofa. (Damn, when will you stop whoring? Or are you after social grants?)[26]

Or imagine a young man talking to his grandpa about a conference centre that's just opened in the neighbourhood (yes, we have those in the townships):

GRANDPA: Kwenzakalani kuleli bhilidi elisha, ohlala uya kulo (What happens in that new building you always go to)?

GRANDSON: Kuya mithwa, mkhulu (Meetings happen there, Grandpa).

GRANDPA: Hayi bo, ngezikhathi zethu, leyonto sasiyenzela ekameleni. Nina ma min'emnyama ninemihlolo. 'Yaz nizofa. (WTF? In our time, such things happened in the bedroom. You millennials are up to shit.)

What a mess.

---

26 Black grannies are blunt like this. It's probably from having to deal with all that apartheid.

Melusi
on Everyday Life
(as a Twenty-First-Century Zulu Man)

▼▲▼

Navigating life as a twenty-first-century African is interesting, to say the least. It definitely isn't anything like what our parents lived through.

It's a brave new world. Are you brave enough to give it a go? I know I am; this is the time and place to be.

BINGELELA

Bingelela is to greet.

Greeting is an important part of acknowledging one another's existence. But it can easily get too much, especially in the workplace. Walking from one part of the building to another, two black friends, who also happen to be colleagues, walk past a third black colleague. Only one of the friends greets the third colleague.

FRIEND 1: You didn't greet Jabu.

FRIEND 2: And?

FRIEND 1: Are you two having issues?

FRIEND 2: No.

FRIEND 1: So, why didn't you greet him?

FRIEND 2: Because I greeted him earlier in the day.

FRIEND 1: I also greeted him earlier in the day, but as a people we greet each other every time, especially when we know each other. Otherwise … otherwise it just looks wrong.

FRIEND 2: Looks wrong se gat. Maybe back in the day, when we had land, we'd bingelela each other every time we saw each other because we didn't see each other so damn often. I'd see you in the morning, as we headed off to work our respective pieces of land then we'd greet each other again at the end of the day, if we hadn't been killed by wild animals. Now we're in office buildings. I can't greet you every time I see you at the copier, in the kitchen, at a meeting, at the water cooler, in the loo.

FRIEND 1 (unconvinced): Hmmm.

ISIKHATHI

Isikhathi is time.

No, not African time, because there is no such thing as African time. There is just plain old time. Actually, scrap that. Time is definitely old, but it certainly is not plain. Far from it, in fact. Time quickly becomes a very complex thing when people start abusing it.

There is I-don't-respect-myself-so-there-is-no-way-I-would-respect-you-or-your-time time. That's not African time. It's asshole time. Some Africans are assholes. But every population group has its fair share of assholes with this attitude.

There is I-picked-up-the-most-beautiful-boy-in-world-last-night-so-I-had-to-get-it-all-this-morning-twice time. That is also not African time. It's I-gots-to-get-mine time. We've all been there. If you haven't, askies.

Then you get my-children-are-shits time. And there is I-forgot-my-wallet-in-my-other-pants-and-I-have-to-drive-back-and-get-it time. Once again, not African time.

There is oh-my-God-my-period-just-started-and-I-am-not-wearing-a-pad time. Nah, that's not African time. It's a part of life. Deal with it.

(Isikhathi is also the isiZulu word for period. It's definitely isikhathi for government to heed society's calls for the supply of free pads and tampons to underprivileged girls and women.)

There is I-forgot-to-put-on-lotion-and-now-I-am-mpunga-so-I-am-gonna-go-back-home-and-apply-lotion time. Not African time. Just mpunga[27] vaarbs.

There is I-am-not-getting-into-that-taxi-alone-because-those-men-look-suspicious time. Also not African time. We just live in a horrifying world.

There is even-though-I-live-50-km-away-from-work-and-have-to-wake-up-at-04:30-every-morning-get-the-kids-ready-then-take-a-bus-and-a-taxi-to-get-to-work-I-am-always-on-time-but-today-the-taxi-I-was-in-got-impounded-because-it-was-not-roadworthy-and-the-replacement-taxi-took-forever-to-arrive-actually-you-know-what-screw-you time. This is not African time.

There is do-I-really-have-to-go-to-this-meeting-that-should-have-been-an-e-mail time. Again, not African time. It's just impossible to walk fast when you're dragging yourself.

I could go on and on. The point is that isikhathi is the isiZulu word for time.

---

27 Mpunga is grey. See 'Mpunga', p. 184

While you're here, can we talk about the eternity that is a black Zionist church service or a black funeral? The funerals are so long I suspect there's a belief that, the longer the funeral, the more likely the deceased is to rise from the dead. Like black people would be able to deal with someone rising from the dead.

Wait a minute. I've just realised there is a conceptual equivalent to what self-righteous assholes call African time. It's how long the Western Cape government knew the water crisis was inevitable before sounding the alarm.

PHOLA

Phola is a verb meaning to heal, cool off, calm down, or relax.

You see, our ancestors were much evolved. They knew that people who lash out or seek to hurt others are, themselves, hurting. That is why the word for healing and calming down is the same.

As a nation, we constantly deal with a lot of hurt and lashing out. That is not about to change, but we can begin to turn the tide by changing the way in which we approach and react to others.

So, let's all phola and encourage others to do the same.

If a cashier screams 'DECLINED!' after you've tried to pay with your card, look her dead in the eyes, smile and then slowly run your finger across your throat while saying, 'Phola, Sathane.'

When a fellow motorist calls you a kaffir because he or she doesn't like something you did (it happens all the fucking time), roll down your window and calmly say, 'Phola, Sathane.'

When the school principal calls you and tells you your child has bitten, beaten, scratched, or tripped another kid, calmly say, 'Phola, dear. Girls will be girls.'

Ladies, when your friend finds out that you slept with her husband, calmly say, 'Phola, choma. You are too good for him anyway.' Then share your champagne with her. Slay!

When a metro cop tries to extort a bribe, pull out your phone, start recording him and say, 'Phola while I record this, chief!'

When a fellow motorist hoots at you because you didn't tear off like Lewis Hamilton as soon as the traffic light turned green, raise your middle finger and mouth the words 'phola, nja' into the rearview mirror.

When your wife whines about her boss, calmly say, 'Phola, I know where he lives. I'll fix this.'

As you can see, phola can help us become the nation we're truly meant to be.

An aside: Growing up as a non-English speaker in a non-English country where the English media dominates can present a few strange moments. For instance, thanks to Christmas advertising, as a child I thought polar bears were phola bears, the most chilled bears in the world. I was under the firm impression that phola bears chilled in the show, ate marshmallows and washed them down with Coca-Cola. That was until I watched a documentary showing polar bears hunting seals. There is absolutely nothing chilled about polar bears. They are anything but phola bears.

ISIBOSHWA

Isiboshwa is a prisoner.

No, this is not about political prisoners or criminals. It's about all of us, and how we've become iziboshwa (plural) in prisons of our own making. I'm talking about WhatsApp groups.

Yes, the family groups, school groups, community groups – they are all prisons and you are isiboshwa. It starts out innocuously enough, and usually with the best intentions. But before you know it, you want out, but cannot leave for fear of judgement and retribution.

I know some say you shouldn't give a damn, and should simply leave. Ya, but those people are psychopaths and would shove their own grandmothers down the staircase for their inheritance – if they haven't done so already.

But if you're a normal person, the idea of pulling out of a group that's meant to serve the greater good is daunting. When you pull out of a community group, how does it not imply that you want other people to ensure that things work well in the community without putting in any work yourself?

If you pull out of a family group, the rest of the group immediately suspects that you think you're better than them and that they bore you. If you pull out of a school or class group, you are a bad, uncaring parent. I am not a member of any religious WhatsApp groups, but I suspect leaving one means you're going to some kind of hell.

So, we remain iziboshwa, bombarded with information we don't care about and that doesn't add any value to our lives.

No, Aunty Sibongile, no one wants to hear about your diarrhoea.

No, Timmy's mom, we don't give a shit about your hippy-dippy parenting advice. BTW, Timmy is not enlightened; my kid says he keeps trying to hump the school rabbits.

Mr Levitan, there are no random black men casing the neighbourhood. Those are your gay Pedi neighbours going for a walk.

#Whatsappgroupsmustfall

ISITHOMBE

Isithombe is a picture.

When some people post their #throwbackthursday pics on social media, you are sometimes left thinking, *Kanti,*[28] *how old are you? That isithombe is from when South Africa was still a union, mos. Jesu wase*[29] *Transvaal Colony, you're old.*

They say isithombe speaks a thousand words. Well, these days, those words are often pure lies. With these phones with filters, you can no longer trust isithombe. Nope. You'll see isithombe of someone you know and you barely recognise them: 'Hey, where are the pimples? When did your cheekbones get such definition? I was with you when you took that pic. That is not how you looked. What witchcraft is this?'

To take a picture is to thwebula, which is also to steal your soul and turn you into a zombie. We've all seen the throngs of people whose souls have been stolen by the selfie culture – Instagram zombies roaming the streets, seeking their next picture-perfect location to take the next selfie. The Council for Giving isiZulu Names and Words to Foreign Words, Concepts and General Foreign Shit (CFGiZNAWTFWCAGFS) got it spot

---

28 See 'Kanti', p. 181.

29 Wase means of, as in 'Jesu of Transvaal Colony'.

on when they gave 'photography' an isiZulu word. A photographer is umthwebuli, which means 'a soul thief'.

BIZA

Biza is to call.

As in, we must stop calling traditional weddings traditional weddings, because then the so-called white wedding should be called a costume party. Yes?

Traditional weddings are simply weddings.

Biza is also a colloquial term for expensive. As in, besides, white weddings abiza unnecessarily.

HLULEKA

Hluleka is to fail.

Elon Musk must talk to me when he invents a phone with a battery that doesn't die. Till then, he's an underachiever. Uyahluleka, Elon.

UMUNTU WESIMAME

Umuntu wesimame is a female – a woman. Umuntu is person. Wesimame (we + simame) means 'of the womenfolk'.

Have you ever heard of umuntu wesimame who spent all her money on fast men? Me neither. Do you know why she doesn't exist? Because abantu besimame (women, plural) are selfish.

Society is obsessed with the men who spend all their money on fast women. And rightly so, because that culture is toxic in so many ways. But can we also talk about the stinginess of abantu besimame? Come on, girls, it's the twenty-first century. Spend your kids' school fees on impressing young guys with champagne at the club. Buy cars you can barely afford just to impress hot boys. You know they love a hot car. Take them on expensive holidays in Dubai, but don't appear in the pics because you have a family who thinks you're away on business.

We need a Mandla Mthembu wesimame to go broke from spending millions on a male Khanyi Mbau. She must lease matching Lamborghinis for herself and her toyboy.

Or is this already happening, but I don't know about it because I am not a hot boy with a sugar mommy? Probably … story of my life.

Abantu is the plural of umuntu. Besimame is the plural of wesimame.

UMCULO

Umculo is music. Oh, sweet, sweet music. Umculo is related to cula, which is to sing.

Does this mean every song (iculo) has to feature a singer? Can you have umculo without ukucula (singing)? Of course you can. In fact, some songs would be so much better if the singers would just shut the hell up.

A song starts, and immediately it grabs your attention. You start bopping your head. *This is my jam*, you think to yourself as your hips start swinging. Good times.

But then, oh no! The godless banshee of a singer or useless rapper pipes up and ruins everything with his or her wailing. We all know songs like that. Even Auto-Tune can't save them.

In the era of style over substance, with singers' looks being more important than talent, it is the lover of umculo who suffers. The very thing that is meant to soothe our souls now grates our nerves.

God, I sound like an old person. So be it, though. I am an old person who now prefers umculo without abaculi (singers). Whenever I hear iculo with an awesome beat being destroyed by a pretty or handsome banshee or mumbler, I seek out the instrumental version and listen to that, filling in the singing bits with the voices in my head – voices that may have devilish thoughts and intentions, but also have the singing voices of angels and the rapping styles of OGs ('original gangsters', Tannie Juanita).

Umculo is dead. Long live umculo.

SEBENZISANA

Sebenzisana is to work together or collaborate.

Musicians do this a lot, especially hip-hop artists. But I've always wondered why, when collaborating on a song, they don't discuss the theme. So often, you'll be listening to a song and you'll realise the artists are not even rapping about the same thing.

Also, if I invite you to feature on my track, and you start rapping about how you're the richest, sexiest, most ill rapper around, you're gonna get punched. It's my damn song. Unless we're rapping about STDs, you're not the most ill; that's me.

You should rap about how grateful you are that I invited you. Or stick to the theme.

UMLILO

Umlilo is fire.

There is no umlilo in hell. Just eternal R&B.

Hell is a horrible place.

GOLOZA

To goloza is to resist, be defiant, or stand your ground.

If former president Zuma could goloza resigning for as long as he did, knowing he was in the wrong, why are you backing down when you're in the right? The man went from Msholozi to #mgolozi.

Take after him and goloza with all your might for what you believe in. Goloza so people don't take advantage of you. Goloza so you get what's due to you. But don't be afraid to goloza purely for control, either.

Your toddler wants to go to crèche in only her undies, with pantihose on her head? Goloza. Don't let her tears move you; definitely don't let your tears distract you.

Goloza.

The crush who's been ignoring you all along is suddenly nice to you in February? Goloza. She just wants a gift on Valentine's Day. You're being used. She can come back after the fourteenth. Goloza.

Your fiancée's family wants fifty cows, two hundred goats, six hundred chickens and a G-Wagen? Goloza. You're not their ticket out of poverty.

Your brand-new girlfriend wants you to buy her hair? Goloza. Whose head is it, kanti?

The queue marshal wants you to sit in the front seat of the

taxi so counting fares can be your problem? Goloza. It's gonna end in tears.

Your brain tells you to leave the house without applying lotion because you're running late? Goloza. You will regret being ashy in public.

Your brain tells you you're not that drunk, so it's okay to drive? Goloza. The brain is a liar – the drunk brain even more so.

The very same drunk brain tells you to dance? Goloza. There is no dancing in church. Maybe movement-nyana, but not full-on getting down.

Your client wants to pay you less than they usually pay other suppliers because you're female/black/young/disabled/a small business? Goloza.

They want to pay you 'in exposure' instead of hard cash? Goloza and walk away.

Your ego wants you to race the Mustang driver who's revving at the traffic lights? Goloza.

Your pastor wants you to eat snakes? Goloza. What the hell is wrong with you?

Your pastor wants to bless your womb with his holy penis? Goloza. Unless you really want his penis inside you. But then just say that's what you want.

A piece of chocolate cake is shaking its ass and beckoning you over? Goloza. You know it's going straight to your hips.

They say the Inuit have a ridiculous number of words for snow. We have just as many for no. When I goloza, I prefer these ones: angifuni, angeke, unyile, uyanya, awunyi perhaps, uyabheda or 'tsek.

SIFELANI?

Sifelani is really more of a rhetorical question than a word. Directly translated, sifelani means 'why are we dying?'

It's the equivalent of the English 'kill me now'. But whereas the English speaker is so bored she'd rather die, the isiZulu speaker wants to know why you are boring her to death. We already have so many things killing us – or trying to. We don't need to count your boring nonsense as one of them.

Take tech, for instance. While it's fantastic and the future really is here, tech has also saddled us with pseudo-futurists who bore us to death. Someone reads a single article about AI and we never hear the end of it. Blah blah blah, automation. Yada yada yada, bot. Seriously? Sifelani?

Yes, yes, your phone has five cameras and one of them takes X-rays. Shut up about it already – sifelani?

You have a self-driving car. Sifelani? BTW, that's just cruise control. A 2008 Camry is not a self-driving car.

The fact that your father and his buddies spent their youth poking one another doesn't mean they predicted Facebook. Sifelani?

Elon Musk this. Elon Musk that. He was born in Tshwane. You were born in Tshwane. Yoooh. Sifelani?

But it's not only pseudo-futurists who are boring us to death.

Gluten (whatever the hell that is) is the true enemy. Sifelani?

You recycle? We know. Sifelani?

But sifelani doesn't only apply to boring stories. You can use it to express your unhappiness about almost anything.

Tax increases? Sifelani?

Fuel levy hike? Sifelani?

More sin tax increases? Sifelani?

They're killing us, here – fi fi fi fi.

UYAHLUPHA

Uyahlupha means 'to be troublesome', or 'he or she is trouble-some', depending on the intonation when pronouncing the 'u'.

For instance, we were out for a drink when a posh, gin-drinking friend of mine started his nonsense. This man uyahlupha.

> POSH BROTHER TO BARMAN: May I have a swizzle stick?
>
> (Barman hands him a straw.)
>
> POSH BROTHER TO ME (aghast): This is a straw. I asked for a swizzle stick!
>
> ME: Just stir with the straw.
>
> POSH BROTHER: Are we savages, Mshengu?[30] Is this what our people died for?
>
> ME: Uyahlupha.
>
> POSH BROTHER: I have rights, Donga. Rights.

It was a very long night.

INTELEZI

Intelezi is a concoction used to cleanse aura, and chase away bad spirits and bad luck. Intelezi keeps you safe as you walk through the valley of death that is life. It gets rid of isinyama.[31]

Intelezi is not imbiza.[32] Imbiza cleanses your insides, while intelezi deals with outside forces. The ANC has been in need of very strong intelezi for a really long time. Same with Parliament.

---

30 Mshengu and Donga are part of the Tshabalala clan praises.

31 Isinyama is a dark cloud – bad luck. Isinyama is related to mnyama – darkness. Mnyama is not meat; that's nyama.

32 A herbal cure; see 'Imbiza', p. 124.

There has never been a better time than right now for an intelezi cleansing.

It's not just our politicians who need intelezi.

Your Phuza Thursday one-night stand has just left your place? Sprinkle intelezi around the flat. Don't forget to add some to your bath water.

You've been in a room with Helen Zille? Intelezi spritz definitely needed before you interact with the rest of society.

You were 'blessed' by a Zupta? You know what to do.

You repaid the Zupta in kind? Spray intelezi on your privates and backside. Three times a day. For a week. Don't forget to gargle. You will also need an intense imbiza regimen.

You're submitting a tender and don't have a 'connection' in Procurement? Spray your submission with intelezi.

Your kid is going for her driving test and has not paid a bribe? Tell her to ditch the perfume and go with intelezi.

Your crush is finally your bae? Spray him with intelezi to get rid of the ex's essence.

Spray intelezi into the Uber before entering. Sprinkle some around a new office. Spritz it around your new lover's place, especially the bed.

Intelezi is life, y'all.

KANTI

Kanti is pretty versatile. It can mean 'after all', 'then', 'in fact', 'whereas', 'so', 'actually' and 'but'. It can also be used as a stand-alone question, and so much more. Here are a few examples of its use:

FRIEND 1: He acted like he loved me kanti that Sathane

just wanted me for my body. Kanti, I also just wanted him for his body.

FRIEND 2: Kanti, you're both rubbishes.

FRIEND 1: Kaaaanti.

Kanti why do you care whether Friend 1 and Friend 2 are two women, two gay men, a gay man and a woman, or whether they are cisgender or non-binary? Kanti, what's wrong with you?

Here's another scenario. Your wife asks you to cook when you get home because you'll be home before her. She gets home and finds you eating pizza while playing FIFA.

WIFE: Kanti?

YOU: Kanti, what?

WIFE: Kanti, why didn't you cook?

YOU: Kanti, you no longer love pizza.

WIFE: Kanti, why are you like this? You know I do. Move over and hand me a controller so I can kick your ass.

For effect, you can also use kanti in an incomplete sentence.

FRIEND 1: I thought my new girlfriend wasn't racist, kaaaaanti …

FRIEND 2: Noooooo, not Sandy.

FRIEND 1: Kanti, not only is she not racist, she can also dance.

Different scenario:

FRIEND 1: I thought my boss was a perfect gentleman, kaaaaanti …

FRIEND 2: Men are trash.

FRIEND: Kanti, why are they such trash?

FRIEND 2: Kanti, who raised them.

Kanti, when are you going to get off Facebook and focus on driving?

CHAZA

In one context, chaza means to impress, charm, or amuse. In another, it means to explain. There is a difference in the pronunciation.

For instance, you walk into one of those workout classes favoured by women. You see a couple of heavyset sisters, so you think, *Yeah, I'm in the right class. I am safe here.* A short while in, you're huffing and puffing, wishing your mother would magically appear and whisk you away; the big queens are steaming ahead. WTF?

The sisters see you suffering and it chazas them. They taunt you: 'Woza, bhuti. Woza. Don't give up.'

While their words are encouraging, you know deep down they are thinking, *Woo, this must be one of those one-round brothers. Poor wife.*

Now you're tempted to chaza yourself to them. You want to chaza that you have high blood pressure and your doctor told you take it easy. You want to chaza that you're a beast in bed, though, and the wife is more than satisfied. Your prowess chazas her.

I honestly don't know why I keep doing this to myself. Someone must chaza this to me.

UMFAZI

Umfazi is a woman or wife.

Growing up, I would hear older Zulu men say that the word umfazi means she who dies with the truth (um = one who, fa = dies, zi = knowing). I never used to pay this chauvinist nonsense any mind. But then Mzansi Magic brought *Utatakho* to our TV screens.[33]

Hayi bo. What in the actual fuck? Bo mama, benenzani (Mother, what were you up to)? Was it apartheid that got you all twisted? Was it migrant labour?

The grown children who take their elderly parents to *Utatakho* are also nuts. Your life is not falling apart because you don't know who your father is. It's not the ancestors on your father's side reaching out to you. Your life is falling apart because you're on drugs and commit crime. Stop those two things and you'll see how much better your life will be.

Yoh, *Utatakho* has jaded me. In fact, at one point I decided to stop watching it because it had me side-eyeing my lovely kids. But I couldn't.

Utatakho brings home the sad reality of South Africa's absent fathers. It is heartbreaking to see how many people grow up without their dads. But what's even sadder is that this nonsense continues to this day. Young men still run, leaving women to raise kids alone, often at the expense of their education.

We need to do better.

MPUNGA

Mpunga means ashy, as in the colour a dark-skinned black person's skin takes when it's too dry.

Yooooooh ... you white people, light-skinned coloureds, Indians (not the black-people-with-weaves Indians) and yellow bones, you have no idea. None at all. You will never, ever,

---

33 For a short explanation of the TV show *Utathako*, see 'Ufuzo' on p. 103.

fully comprehend the mpunga struggle we darker berries have to deal with. Your skin merely gets dry; we become mpunga.

We can call ourselves melanin warriors, or melanin queens, or whatever, but being mpunga is the bane of our existence. If we're not careful, it can – and sometimes does – derail our lives.

You're running late one morning, so you forget to apply lotion, or you don't apply it properly. While driving, you notice your hands are ashy, especially between the fingers. Nooooooo! Umpunga.

You're really late – too late to turn back or stop at a garage to buy lotion. But you can't go to your meeting because you're fucking mpunga. Maybe you should just drive into oncoming traffic and end it all. No one will notice how mpunga you are when you're bleeding out.

You get out of a swimming pool and realise you have no lotion. Shiiiiiit. Why are these waters not shark-infested? At least then you could jump back in so the sharks could put you out of your misery. The fact that swimming pools make you mpunga is probably why so many black people don't swim, especially at pool parties. I don't want to find myself having to use the host's lotion, which is probably lavender-scented.

I know of darker people who have had to turn down sex offers from their dream lovers, because sex would mean getting naked and they had done a hasty job of applying lotion that morning. This is a particularly big problem in winter. So, if you're planning on seeing a dark person naked in winter, you'd better tell them the night before, so they know to suffer the cold in the morning and apply lotion liberally.

If we're married to you, sorry for you – you will see us in all our ashy glory. We're not suffering winter mornings for you.

Khethile, khethile. Ngenile, ngenile. Shadile, shadile.[34] (You've made your bed, now lie in it with your mpunga spouse.)

BTW, the winter mpunga struggle is how a good friend of mine got himself kicked out of the marital home. His wife noticed that he'd started applying lotion to his whole body on winter mornings. That's when she knew that someone else was seeing him naked.

HEH, BANTU

Heh, bantu expresses shock and surprise. It's similar to 'what the hell?' Bantu is people, but can specifically mean black people (although not in a negative, colonial context). So, when you say, 'Heh, bantu,' you're asking other people if they are seeing, hearing, or experiencing what you are seeing, hearing, or experiencing – or you're asking them to help you make sense of what is happening.

The night we watched Lindiwe Zulu on eNCA taking part in a civil discussion instead of swearing and screaming, as she does in Parliament, there was a collective heh, bantu.

When a parking attendant wants you to pay him for helping you get out of a parking spot you were perfectly capable of getting out of on your own because you're a grown-up with a legitimate driver's licence, heh, bantu.

When the Checkers cashier shouts, 'Your card was declined. It doesn't have money, bhuti,' even though it's the Speedpoint that's faulty, heh, bantu.

---

34 Khethile means you have chosen. Ngenile means you are in. Shadile means you are married. Put together, these mean, 'You have made your choice and can't get out of this marriage.'

When someone inboxes you on Facebook to say nothing but 'hi' over and over, heh, bantu. Futsek.

When listening to a Steve Komphela post-match interview, heh, bantu of the people of the bantu.

What they did to Mama Winnie Mandela, heh, bantu.

When grown men with beards call me uncle, heh, bantu.

When someone says they can't cook, heh, bantu.

When you are called a reverse racist for confronting racism, heh, bantu.

When, as men, we are more upset by #menaretrash than the actions of other men, heh, bantu.

When Nando's charges an arm, a leg, a kidney and half your spleen for a quarter chicken and chips, heh, bantu.

When people at the office believe their preferred aircon settings suit everybody, heh, bantu.

Co-workers, heh, bantu.

Employers, heh, bantu.

Employees, heh, bantu.

Clients, heh, bantu.

Fellow motorists, heh, bantu.

Pedestrians, heh, bantu.

Children, heh, bantu.

Parents, heh, bantu.

Relatives, heh, bantu.

The police, heh, bantu.

Lovers, heh, bantu.

Politicians, heh, bantu.

South Africa, heh, bantu.

South Africans, heh, bantu.

The ANC, heh, bantu.

Helen Zille, heh, bantu.

You could also say 'heh, madoda', but down with patriarchy – so, we stick with 'heh, bantu'. Madoda is men.

SHEBA and ISISHEBO

These are not related to the Sesotho 'sheba' (look or watch). They relate to food, eating, and more.

While isishebo has been used by opportunistic food brands to brand sauces and other concoctions targeted at black people, its root word, sheba, is not really familiar outside South African black culture. Sheba is the verb – the thing you do. Isishebo is the noun – the thing you do the action with.

In the context of eating, to sheba is to supplement your staple or starch with isishebo (savoury elements) like meat, gravy, veggies and sauces (usually, there's some kind of protein in the mix).

Isishebo is a big deal, okay? It can end friendships and relationships. The isishebo you prepare and dish up can be an indicator of your socioeconomic standing. The isishebo you serve me tells me what you think of me.

Tread carefully, here: offering to cook for a prospective lover can be a risky business because of isishebo politics. Rather stick to restaurants; then, the isishebo politics isn't your problem. Even then, you could still get dumped if the person believes you chose a particular restaurant to insult their isishebo world view, or that the choice of restaurant reflects your isishebo world view, which they think is a disgusting one.

Another crucial aspect is how you deal with your isishebo. Do you eat it first, then move on to the starch? Or do you eat them together? This could tell a prospective lover what you are like in bed, or give prospective in-laws an idea of how you will treat their daughter or son.

The isishebo issue can also affect how lobolo negotiations go, or whether you get the contract or the place in the team or choir. How religions' rules impact on isishebo affects religious choices in turn: some religions dictate what you can and can't use as isishebo.

That isishebo is so important doesn't mean that starch isn't, though. In your relationships, it's important to know whether you're the isishebo or the starch. Two izishebo can be messy, while two starches suck: imagine eating pap with rice. This is not a sexual orientation thing. It applies to many things. In short, opposites attract.

Weekends are isishebo and December is isishebo.

VOVA

Vova is to wring and strain, which is an important step in making traditional (sorghum) beer.

As part of the beer-making process, fermented sorghum[35] sludge is poured into a sheath, which is then wrung. The beer strains out of the porous contraption, leaving the fermented sorghum behind. That is ukuvova (to wring and strain).

Ukuvova inkani is what happens to people in a similar process. Inkani is obstinacy; ukuvova inkani is to wring a person until the stubbornness strains out of them, leaving them spent.

---

35 Sorghum is amabele, which is the same word as for breasts, only pronounced slightly differently.

This is a technique favoured by some of South Africa's – and maybe even the world's – most hard-core negotiators, people who go into a situation without any intention of yielding. The only outcome that will make them happy is seeing you reduced to a trembling mess of snot and tears. Practitioners of this technique independently decide that you have inkani, and that it's their divine duty to vova it out of you.

Yep, you guessed it: I'm talking about toddlers and taxi drivers.

While most people have, at some point in their lives, been brought to the verge of tears by a toddler, if you've never taken a taxi you won't fully grasp what ukuvova inkani is. If you think taxi drivers are a nightmare for you as a motorist, you know nothing.

Have you ever experienced a taxi stopping mid-trip with the driver refusing to continue because the fare is 20c short? You're sitting in the front and need to get to madam's house, because she loses her temper if you're even a split second late. So, you offer to cover the 20c.

Now, the driver starts chastising you for trying to protect a dishonest Sathane. The kid, who is heading to a job interview that could change his life, is genuinely 20c short, so he is not going to own up. Having seen how you got chastised, no one else is going to offer either.

Stalemate; the vova-ing[XI] commences.

The taxi driver has vova-ed all of you before he eventually listens to the pleas of an older gentleman. You're already ten minutes late, and the madam can't wait to take her turn to vova you. Shoo. It could drive a person to drink.

If any taxi drivers or madams are reading this post, please go easy on our people.

Other practitioners of this technique are teenagers, cops, estate security guards and body corporate or trustee oumas.

ISISHIMANE

Isishimane is a man who is unlucky, or maybe just shy, with women. Or men. Yes, there are gay izishimane (plural) too.

I once asked my grandma (may she rest in peace) why isishimane sounds so similar to the Sesotho word for boy (moshimane). She said, 'Have you seen Sotho boys? If you are isishimane, you're like a moshimane.' She then laughed until tears rolled down her cheeks. uGogo was a riot, and a total Zulu fundamentalist.

The person who is always the most broke in January is a Shelington[36] sishimane. He spent too much in December, shem. As we all know, being a Shelington doesn't guarantee you success with the ladies.

Izishimane grow up to be blessers, and gold diggers are their saving grace. So, don't knock gold diggers: they are doing the Lord's work.

Ladies, if you're married to a man who was isishimane growing up, you are in trouble when he starts making money. He is going to show you flames making up for his lost youth. He is going to be a blesser. But because once a isishimane, always a sishimane, the little girls are playing him.

Now your isishimane husband is on the couch sulking, and

---

36 See 'Shela', p. 111.

you think it's something you did. It's got nothing to do with you: the girl he took to Durban July won't return his calls. Bloody popeye.[37]

DINA

If you hear um'Zulu mention your name and the word 'dina' in the same sentence, and there is no 'i', 'u' or 'ku' in front of it, it is unlikely that he is thinking about inviting you for dinner and maybe sexy time afterwards. In fact, you'll probably never get that invitation, even if *you* threw in the idea of sexy time. Okay, maybe if the sexy time is a guarantee, part of a binding contract. But it's a very slim chance.

Since we Zulufy some English words, dina could mean dinner. But when your name is mentioned in the same sentence as dina, it's likely you're being called a special kind of irritating. Dina means both to irritate and to tire out.

Uyadina. Uyisidina – you're a drag. You're draining.

If there was an 'i', 'u' or 'ku' in front of the dina, maybe the person was talking about dinner after all. That would be idina – dinner, udina – dinner, kudina – to dinner or at dinner. But it's more likely he was saying udinaaa – he, she, or it is such a draaaaaag. Or maybe he said idinaaa – he or she is such a draaaaag. He could even have said kudinaaa – he, she, or it is such a draaaaaag. The way in which he said the words could have led you to believe he was excited about the prospect of dinner with you.

He isn't.

---

37 See 'Popeye', p. 23.

So many things dina us. Especially corporate life. That's why we like Dizemba so much. We are tired from izidina that we have to deal with throughout the year.

As I write this, I'm thinking of all the things that dina me. I kept shaking my head and saying 'yeses'. Now, I don't want to go to work.

iTraffic idinaaa.

Messed-up traffic lights adinaaa.

Newspaper vendors badinaaa.

Roadblocks in the morning adinaaa.

Taxi drivers badinaaa.

People who try to hide their asshole behaviour behind not having had their morning coffee badinaaa.

Amaphotocopier adinaaa.

Projectors adinaaa.

Forms adinaaa.

Impossible deadlines adinaaa.

iSARS idinaaa.

Dropping the kids off at school kudinaaa.

NTWASAHLOBO

Ntwasahlobo is spring (the season).

The beginning of the South African ntwasahlobo is great because it contains both the brutal, humbling honesty of winter and the bright enthusiasm of summer in three happy weeks of delusion. You forget that winter froze your left testicle off and that summer wants to grill your soul.

Autumn is ntwasabusika. Summer is hlobo. Winter is busika.

UKUHLANYA

Ukuhlanya means 'to go crazy' or 'madness'. The root word is hlanya (to go crazy/insane). No, not ihlaya – that's 'joke'.

Whenever we switch from summer to autumn and the temperatures begin to drop, ukuhlanya starts to rear its ugly head. Nothing highlights this madness like the Great Office Aircon Wars. These wars start early in March and last until deep into September, with the most brutal skirmishes taking place in June and July.

That is seven months of ukuhlanya, or more than half the year. During this period, colleagues who are usually cordial to one another are at one another's throats. There's name-calling. Plotting. Conspiracies. Tears. Lots of chattering teeth.

You see, at the beginning of March, some people start wearing boots, long johns and electrically heated onesies to the office already because of the ukuhlanya of office aircon wars. For as long as South Africans continue to work in air-conditioned offices, this country will never know peace. Forget land: aircon is the real fly in the rainbow-coloured ointment.

It's ukuhlanya.

Outside the office, this drop in temperature helps some of us acclimatise to the ukuhlanya that is shopping at Woolies. In summer, the difference between atmospheric temperature and Woolies temperature makes it too risky to waltz in there without a jacket. Add to that the damage it does to your pocket, and the listeriosis scandal, and shopping at Woolies proves ukuhlanya all year round.

So, fellow South Africans, I implore you to think carefully before reaching for the aircon settings at work between March and September. This is a sensitive time. Managers and company owners: you may be in charge, but that doesn't mean the temperatures you find comfortable work for everyone else. That kind of thinking is ukuhlanya.

Melusi's Everyday Advice

▼▲▼

There is nothing I dislike more than unsolicited advice. Okay, I lie: there are things I dislike more, but unsolicited advice is right up there with the things I dislike most.

I will completely understand, then, if you don't take any of the advice in this section. In fact, I'd recommend that you ignore most of it. I have been known to lead people astray. I was that kid with whom the other kids were told not play. Rather just focus on learning the isiZulu words and expressions.

ISIBUKO

Isibuko is a mirror.

The word is related to buka, which means to look at. Isibuko is the thing you use to look at yourself.

As a country, we need a collective isibuko. We need to take a long, hard look at ourselves. Then, we need to be honest with ourselves about who we are and what we want, because it all starts with the man or woman in the isibuko.

Do you like what you see? No, not the eyebrows on fleek, your stylish goatee, or your phuza face. What you see on the inside. Does it make you happy? Is it something you want to bring into our Zumaless world?

Whether you are pro- or anti-Zuma, it doesn't matter. He is gone. We have a new president. There is a buzz, a sense of optimism, in the air. When you look into isibuko, do you see someone who is going to ride that wave and try to play their part in helping build a better South Africa? I hope so.

Of course, it won't be easy. It will continue to feel as if our efforts mean nothing in the greater scheme of things. But what we do does matter. It really, really does.

Here's the thing: we don't spend every day with the president or politicians. They are not the people with whom we work or do business. They are not the teachers in our children's schools. They are not the motorists with whom we share our roads.

It's not the president who pees on the toilet seat and doesn't wipe it. (Maybe he does; it could be the one thing Cyril's wife hates most about him.)

It's not the mayor who chews with his mouth open. (Maybe Patricia de Lille does; that could be the real reason they were trying to get rid of her.)

It's not the minister of finance who plays Candy Crush on his employer's time. (Oh, wait. It is. Ah, well. You know what I mean.)

It's not Julius Malema who doesn't yield for fellow motorists. (I bet Julius is *such* a courteous driver.)

It's not Hellen Zille who farts in a taxi. (But I bet she would.)

It's not Jeff Radebe who catcalls women on the street. He just sends texts, requesting C.l.i.t.

It's not Kenneth Meshoe of the Anti-Christ Devil's Pal (ACDP) who eats people's leftovers without asking.

What I am saying is, it's the man or woman in the mirror who ruins our day. So, why not simply stop being an idiot and try to be a better person?

LILIZELA

Lilizela is to ululate, which is done in celebration.

It irritates usathane and jealous neighbours. In fact, I am certain the first ancestor to lilizela did so specifically to irritate a hater neighbour who was not happy about her daughter marrying a sexy Tshabalala man. And boy, did the neighbour get pissed off.

First, because it wasn't her daughter who was getting married to the Tshabalala stallion. Second, because ukulilizela was so damn loud and piercing that whole year. The jealous neighbour was so angry that she became the first ancestor to adopt a white surname when the settlers arrived. She then moved in with amaXhosa and the trend took hold.

Here's the thing, though. We shouldn't only celebrate the truly magical stuff, like marrying a Tshabalala man. Let's cherish the little victories, too.

You managed to parallel park in under an hour. Lilizela.

Your boyfriend managed to pee without splashing all over the toilet seat. Lilizela.

You opened a can of cooldrink without breaking your gel-tipped nail or having to ask a strange man to do it for you, thus running the risk of his stalking you. (Yes, some guys take any interaction initiated by a woman as a come-on.) Lilizela, gherl.

You managed to hold your tongue when your stupid boss was being a dumbass. Again. Lilizela.

You ate a meal your mother-in-law cooked without getting food poisoning. Lilizela.

You farted in the lift and managed to reach your floor without anyone else getting in. Lilizela.

You changed your kid's diaper without the kid shitting mid-change. Lilizela.

You came home from work to find that no one had eaten the leftovers you'd been dreaming about the whole day. Lilizela.

You're halfway through January and you haven't had to sell a kidney to afford petrol. Lilizela.

You're halfway through January. Lilizela.

Bafana didn't qualify for this year's World Cup in Russia, so you can watch the world's greatest sporting tournament anxiety-free. Lilizela. The bastards.

We don't know what's in store for us with Cyril at the helm of a still-rotten ANC. But we lilizela, because surely it will be better than it was under you-know-who.

Seriously, though. There is so much ugliness that is out of our hands. Let's try to drown it in positive vibes. Sure, we must confront bullshit wherever it raises its ugly head, but let's not forget to lilizela whenever we encounter goodness.[38] Remember, it pisses off usathane. Alilililililili.

HLAFUNA

Hlafuna is to chew.

American pills must be delicious. On TV and in movies, they just hlafuna them. No water, nothing. Hmmmm.

---

38 To my Zimbabwean friends: don't lilizela every time you encounter Goodness. It will piss her off. No, I am not saying she is usathane. What I mean is … Argh, never mind.

Bringing it closer to home, I think South Africa has the world's highest number of people who hlafuna with their mouths open. It's disgusting.

Whether you're at a braai, a stadium, the office, a fast food outlet, a fancy restaurant, or at home, there is always someone chewing with their mouth open. Argh.

Then you've got the ones who eat during meetings, knowing very well that they are going to need to speak. Now he's speaking and hlafuna-ing while the rest of us are on the verge of throwing up. For this reason, snacks should be banned from meetings.

People just aren't mature enough for that kind of responsibility. I am, but nobody else.

VALELA NGAPHANDLE

Valela ngaphandle is to shut out (valela = shut, ngaphandle = outside or outdoors).

If someone doesn't want to give you access to something, they valela you ngaphandle. Which is exactly what is happening to Idris Elba. Idris deserves better roles. Why wasn't he Vibranium in *Black Panther*? Hollywood must stop with the valela ngaphandle.

As human beings, we like to valela ngaphandle, though, don't we? It's our favourite pastime. Racism, sexism, xenophobia, homophobia and many other -isms and phobias are all because of our obsession with shutting one another out.

Imagine the potential lost to the massive valela ngaphandle sessions that were slavery and apartheid. Millions and millions of black people denied the opportunity to reach their full potential and contribute meaningfully to the world. Just imagine how much further humanity would have come had all those people been allowed to thrive.

We can never allow humanity to valela anyone ngaphandle like that ever again. Everyone needs to be free to be themselves and live their best lives. We'll all be better for it.

IVUKUVUKU

Ivukuvuku is the word for a scruffy person. The word is onomatopoeia for the sound made by stuff that flaps about, such as loose-fitting clothes or dreadlocks – it goes 'vuku vuku'.

Vukuzela is the verb. A vukuvuku vukuzelas. I meet so many vukuvukus who are vukuzela-ing all over the place that I have coined a phrase to describe it: deja vukuvuku, the unsettling feeling that you've seen this vukuvuku before.

Parents favour the word, using it to chastise their children when they fail to understand their children's sense of style.

Now, to be clear, being ivukuvuku is not necessarily a bad thing, especially if you're ivukuvuku by choice and it makes you happy. It can be liberating just to be.

We need places for people just to be.

What do we want?

To vukuzela!

When do we want it?

Right now!

As onomatopoeia, vukuvuku is related to s'vunguvungu, which is the isiZulu word for whirlwind. A whirlwind goes vungu vungu as it spins and spins.

Another word related onomatopoeically is vuvuzela. A vuvuzela goes vuuuu vuuuu. Vuvuzela is traditionally a verb.

HABE

Habe is an expression of shock and surprise. It is pronounced 'ha beh'.

It reminds me of the time I started a business with a rather strange guy. There were three of us, yet he wanted us to have a ManCo (management committee), an OpCo (operations committee) and an ExCo (executive committee). He then wanted us to have separate meetings for all these committees. We wouldn't be allowed to discuss stuff pertaining to one committee during another committee's meeting. Habe!

If someone makes a ridiculous request or demand, you can also respond using habe – especially when you have no idea why they would even begin to think you would agree or oblige.

A colleague says you should speak English because she doesn't understand your language, even though you were not even talking to her: habe!

A metro cop says you must give him 'cooldrink', even though you're willing to take the ticket: habe!

Your traitor son says you must take him to the stadium to watch Orlando Pirates, even though he is the only one in the family who doesn't support Kaizer Chiefs: habe!

Your neighbour wants you to continue giving him lifts to work, even though he doesn't contribute towards petrol: habe!

A potential client wants you to do work on spec and, if she likes it, she'll pay you: habe!

The president wants to thuma[39] you but his government has raised VAT and taxes so we have less money and can't afford the petrol to run his errands: habe!

---

39 See 'Thuma', p. 56.

A colleague expects you to greet him every time you bump into him in the corridor, kitchen, boardroom, bathroom and anywhere else: habe!

Never be shy to say habe when people are being unreasonable. Whether it's in your work life or private life, people must know when you're unhappy about their actions.

Habe!

HLEBA

Hleba is to whisper or gossip, or to bad-mouth someone.

When you call a friend to hleba but her phone is off, that's God telling you to stop your nonsense, you spawn of Satan.

AMAGWALA

Gwala is a coward. The plural is amagwala.

Here is an example of its use. People need to go really far back when they pray to their ancestors. You can't pray to these apartheid ones, who keep saying, 'Hayi, mntwana wami. Yeka izinto zabelungu. (No, my child, leave white people's things alone).'

Amagwala.

AMANGA

Amanga means lies.

When someone is lying, you say unamanga. Unamanga literally means you are, or he or she is, full of lies. It is also a way of describing a habitual liar. For instance, 'That Van Breda kid unamanga.'

You can also say ukhuluma (speak or talk) amanga – you're

telling lies. Or uqamba (invent or compose) amanga – you're composing lies.

I like uqamba amanga because there is magic in a well-composed lie. It's a thing of beauty – much like a painting, whose artist will find fame and fortune only after she dies because art is a dicey career choice that should only be pursued by trust fund babies.

It's important to note that there is no singular form of amanga; it's always plural because you can never tell just one lie. Even if it seems you told only one lie, the work that went into it is full of other lies, if only those you may have told yourself. Furthermore, to keep that lie going, you will also have to tell other lies.

Lies are wonderful things: they keep the peace, they comfort, they excite, they motivate, and they keep hope alive. While truth is obviously extremely important and lies can be damaging, lies honestly don't get their due respect as the glue that often keeps our lives from falling apart.

Imagine what a crazy, ridiculous place the world would be if we told the truth all the time. In fact, I doubt there'd still be a world; we would have killed one another a long time ago. I know I'd definitely be dead if I told the complete truth, even for one day. Simple questions like, 'Melusi, what do you think of my (anything)?' would lead to instant death.

Related words demonstrate the importance and magic of lies.

Isimangaliso is a miracle. You immediately know why amanga are part of miracles. Miracles require a suspension of disbelief and are often downright lies. Because we're a practical people, I believe the Zulu ancestors knew to remind us to take miracles with a pinch of salt.

The related isimanga (a phenomenon or strange event) even sounds like a polite way of saying, 'You're a damn liar, but you know what, I need to believe this because my life sucks right now and I'll cling to anything that gives me hope. But if I die from this incurable disease, I'm haunting you first, bitch.'

Manga is also in mangaza, which is to shock, surprise, or amaze. A surprise party without amanga is just a plain old party. Another reason why lies are often necessary and important.

INKANI

Inkani is the only thing they test for at taxi driver school. They don't care if you can drive, know the rules of the road, can count, or even if you have arms or legs. No, it's all about inkani. Whether you have it or not. The more the better.

The School for Townhouse Complex Security Guards also uses the nkani-o-meter to test candidates. In case, you're still wondering, inkani is stubbornness. Pig-headedness.

Speaking of heads, I was recently told that the size of a person's forehead is directly proportional to their level of inkani. I believe this because I have a few friends with massive foreheads and you can't tell them anything. They do whatever they like, whenever they like. In fact, they'll do something just because they were told they shouldn't do it. They'll do it even if they don't really enjoy doing that thing, just so they can satisfy their nkani.

Inkani is a thing that ends friendships, marriages, and even lives. As we saw with the sentencing of one Lady Moemishberg, it can also get you locked up. It wasn't her racism that got that woman convicted and sentenced. It was inkani. Had she just backed down and apologised, even if she didn't mean it, she'd be walking free, able to offend many more people. But noooooo, she had to have inkani.

You lose sight of yourself when you're caught in a fatal inkani spiral. It manifests as so many righteous feelings. It is only when you're in a jail cell full of criminal k@!@#$ who want to vova your nkani that you realise, 'Shit, I fucked up.'

Ladies and gents, let's check our nkani at the door.

ILUNGELO

Ilungelo is a right. Not right as in the opposite of left or the opposite of wrong. A right as in being entitled to do something.

Right, as in the opposite of left, is sokudla and it relates to the hand you eat with. You see, in ancient times, the Zulu ancestors used to starve lefties to death because only the right-handed had the right to eat. Hectic.

Right, as in the opposite of wrong, is lungile. It's clear how that's related to lungelo.

Amalungelo is the plural – rights.

Each year, on 21 March, South Africans shine a light on the human rights that are enshrined in our Constitution. We honour the scores of people who took on a brutal system and lost their lives in the fight for a society in which all our rights are respected and protected.

On that day in 1960, crowds in Sharpeville marched to the police station to protest against the pass laws. They were fired upon by the police, resulting in hundreds of casualties, including scores of children. Many were shot in the back as they fled.

Many others have been slaughtered during our painful past while fighting for the amalungelo we all enjoy today. Black, coloured, Indian, white, Chinese, young, old – we all owe them. The best way we can repay them is to continue to fight injustice wherever we encounter it and to ensure that, in the pursuit of our own interests and amalungelo, we do not infringe on the amalungelo of others, even if we do not agree with their world view. Not just on Human Rights Day, but every day.

Whenever Human Rights Day comes around, I celebrate – that's my ilungelo. But I never forget what it means and what our responsibility is to protect one another's rights.

NB: If you believe the bit about Zulu ancestors starving lefties to death, you're not right in the head. That said, lefties' rights continue to be infringed upon and that's not right.

OK'SALAYO

Ok'salayo is shorthand for oku salayo, which means 'what remains is'.

It's a usually innocuous expression equivalent to the English 'the fact remains'. However, when used in the right way, it can be a resounding act of defiance. Ok'salayo is most effective when you have been bested because your opponent was right – or simply cleverer, fitter, better looking, richer, etc. than you.

When you find yourself in such a situation, instead of conceding, you should say, 'Ok'salayo.' That allows you to walk away with your head held high.

When a man who has been condemned to death says ok'salayo just before the firing squad pulls the trigger, he goes to his grave having had the last laugh. I always imagine that South African political prisoners would have said it just before being hanged.

Ok'salayo can also be followed by an insult or a swear word. For example, a striker scores a spectacular goal, winning his team the World Cup. The opposing goalkeeper says ok'salayo umubi (umubi = you're ugly – so, 'the fact remains, you are ugly'). The goalie wins.

However, the word is sometimes more effective if you say nothing at all after it. This leaves your opponent hanging, wondering what the hell you meant. He or she might even ask what you mean, whereupon, depending on the situation or your bravery, you can just shrug and say uyazi (you know) or 'tsek.

Go out there and tell life ok'salayo.

UMUTHI

Umuthi is a tree, as well as medicine.

And it's umuthi, with an 'h'. The word 'muti' is not isiZulu; it does not exist in our language. English speakers' pronouncing umuthi 'muti' does not make them the same thing. In fact, in isiZulu these two words do not even sound the same. It's the same error that was made when whoever originally ran the Lotto approved the pay-off line 'Tata machance, tata mamillions', which should have been 'Thatha amachance, thatha amamillion'. SMH.[40]

Umuthi gets a bad rap because of witchcraft, as well as psychopaths and their umuthi ('muti') killings. These psychopaths masquerade as medicine men and women. It's fucking insane. The people who go to these psychopaths for potions are also psychopaths. No one in their right mind would believe that

---

40 Shaking my head.

potions infused with body parts will bring you good luck or protect you. It's evil.

I guess it's a good thing South African English speakers use the word muti so we can separate this nonsense from umuthi, which is also used for healing. Even Panado is umuthi.

Now, this is not to say that non-psychopaths don't use umuthi. Sure, we haven't mastered the Limpopo lightning thing, but we will thakatha you to come nice, using umuthi.

You want a girl to fall in love with you: umuthi.

You want your crush to break up with his woman: umuthi.

You want to get that job: umuthi.

You want your team to prevail: umuthi.

You want to stop your marriage from falling apart: umuthi.

Speaking of marriages not falling apart, you can see a man who's had umuthi used on him. He is content and placid. He is not a purveyor of patriarchy and toxic masculinity. He is definitely not trash.

A man on umuthi gives his entire salary to his wife and she gives him pocket money. He gets told who he can be friends with. She has other lovers; he knows this, and is fine with it. Her cellphone has a password; his doesn't.

A man on umuthi has no idea that he is on umuthi. All he knows is that he loves his wife and he is happy. What's so bad about that?

The way I see it, the only good man is a man who's given umuthi three times a day, with his meals, which he cooks himself. Married women, you must thakatha these bastards. Put them on umuthi drips and the world will be a better place.

Using umuthi on boyfriends is plain witchcraft, though.

When referring to men and suggesting that umuthi should

be used on them, I say 'them' and not 'us' because I am not part of that equation. I am just fine without umuthi.

But wait. What if I am already being fed umuthi and I just don't know it? Oh, Lord.

INKINGA

Inkinga means trouble or problem.

In these tumultuous times, the isiZulu words and phrases that follow could help keep you out of trouble:

Angizingeni (I am not getting involved / I am not interested)

Angifuni (I don't want to)

Angiyi lapho (I'm not going there)

Angeke (never)

Asoze (never)

Heyi (stop that shit)

Amasimba ke la (this is bullshit)

Udakiwe (you're clearly drunk)

Hlukana nami (leave me the hell alone)

Phuma kimi (seriously, leave me alone)

Hayi (hell no)

Ini? (what? or piss off)

Awunyi perhaps (are you shitting me?)

'Tsek (fuck off; this word is not necessarily isiZulu, but it's also not not isiZulu).

When in need, this is how you could use these expressions:

If you're a man and your peers start with their misogyny, tell them, ''Tsek.'

If you're white and your friend / relative / lover / colleague starts with racist bullshit and defends the right to own an apartheid flag, don't just stand there. Say, 'Awunyi perhaps?'

If someone you know starts displaying tribalistic or xeno-phobic tendencies, look them in the eye and say, 'Heyi.'

If you're of a certain age and do not work in entertainment or the media but your inner voice tells you to #fillupany-thing,[41] say, 'Ini?'

If you're a young woman and your friend wants you to go 'eat' some guy's money, tell her, 'Angeke.'

If your friend pulls out a suitcase full of cash along with a few cash-in-transit bags, say 'Amasimba ke la,' and get the hell out of there. Maybe even call the police.

If you're a parent and your child tells you that he or she wants to support a sports team that is not Kaizer Chiefs, flick them on the ear and say, 'Udakiwe.'

If you're drunk and feel the urge to text an ex or crush, tell yourself, 'Hayi!'

If you feel the urge to argue with a troll online, remind your-self, 'Angizingeni.'

MUDLE MALI YAKHE

Mudle is eat him or her (the root word is dla, to eat). Mali is money. Yakhe is his or hers.

So, in English, mudle mali yakhe means to eat her or him, or her or his money. What the hell does that mean? Ah, Eng-lish, once again you fail us with your lack of imagination.

Mudle mali yakhe is an expression used to mock a person who has overindulged and is now suffering the consequences.

---

41 In December 2017, hip-hop artist Cassper Nyovest tried to fill Johannes-burg's FNB Stadium for one of his performances. The attempt trended under the hashtag #fillupfnb.

You could be feeling ill, be making a fool of yourself, getting arrested, etc. But it is all happening because you overindulged.

Thing is, you got your bonus and decided you were gonna chow all the money. You were bragging so much that you became insufferable. You were screaming, 'Phuma kimi. Ngidla imali yami. (Leave me alone. I'm chowing my money.)'

Oho.

Guess what? Now your money is actually chowing you. It is devouring you like you're gogo's custard and jelly. It is scoffing you down like you're stuffed chicken. Which you are.

What people don't understand is that money-eating is governed by Newton's third law – for every action, there is an equal and opposite reaction. You eat the money; the money eats you right back. It then throws you up, all chewed up.

As we celebrate whatever we're celebrating, let us ensure that the words 'mudle mali yakhe' are never directed at us.

YEKA

Yeka means to leave something alone.

Being a sugar daddy is sad. But do you know what's even sadder? Wanting to be one and not being able to afford it.

Leave that shit alone, baba. Next thing, you're not paying school fees, levies, bond, car insurance, medical aid etc. Ignore sugar daddy peer pressure. Maybe your dead grandfather was a sugar daddy, and you want to honour him by being just like him. Well, he wasn't a sugar daddy in the time of LVs, iPhone 10s, Cartier watches and champagne. Apartheid-era sugar daddyship was a cheap affair.

Wena, jy sal kak.

UMALALEVEVA

Umalaleveva is malaria.

This word has always fascinated me because it appears to be Zulufied 'malaria fever', but it isn't. Or is it?

Because of the isiZulu relationship with the letter 'r', malaria fever could be pronounced as 'malalia fever', which sounds very close to 'umalaleveva'. But umalaleveva actually has a real and sensible isiZulu meaning: shiver in your sleep. This, of course, is what happens when you're in the grip of malaria fever and chills. Malale relates to lala (sleep), while ukuveva is to tremble.

But what the hell is going on here? Long before anyone called the disease 'malaria', it was giving Africans shivers in the night? Maybe umalaleveva is the disease's original name and malaria is the derivative?

I don't know. What I do know is that you shouldn't let this day send shivers down your spine. Go out there and get yours, just like the pesky mosquito.

ISITHUNZI

Isithunzi is a shadow, but it also refers to dignity or clout.

It's about the size of the shadow you cast – your area of influence. Anything that's seen to diminish isithunzi sakho (your clout or dignity) is obviously not good.

So, do shorter people have less isithunzi? Do fatter people have more? If you go on a diet, does your isithunzi diminish? Does Khulubuse have more of isithunzi than Thuli Madonsela? Of course he does. He actually casts umthunzi – shade.

The isithunzi we're talking about here is the figurative meaning. However, because both clout and dignity are subjective matters, in some circles a fat cat can be seen to have both literal and figurative isithunzi. The way society has linked isithunzi to money and material possessions is a huge part of why we are in some of the shit we are in. It chomps at the threads of our moral fibre.

It is the reason why executives like Markus Jooste act the way they do and government officials get involved with corruption. Greed has no respect for isithunzi.

That said, poverty continues to be the biggest diminisher of isithunzi. There is no dignity in poverty. The way some of our fellow South Africans live is a crime against humanity. Let us not forget to share what little we may have. And if you can, in any way, help restore someone's sithunzi, even if it's for a short while, do not hesitate to do so.

PS: Isithunzela is a zombie – one who is a shadow of herself. Umthunzi wezi nkukhu means shade of the chickens – deep isiZulu colloquialism for marijuana.

MOSHA

Mosha is to ruin, damage, waste or compromise.

The word sounds very similar to rock music's 'mosh'. In fact, 'mosh' comes from 'mosha'. Here's how it happened. Sometime in the 1980s, two enterprising Zulu women set up a landscaping business and soon secured a contract to maintain the grass at a stadium. They did their work diligently and were very proud.

One weekend, the stadium hosted a rock concert, so the women decided to pop by and check out this music the white people were losing their minds over. When they got there, they were shocked by what was happening. It was savagery. Their beautiful grass had been ruined.

With tears in her eyes, the one entrepreneur turned to her friend and said, 'Labantwana bayamosha (These kids are ruining everything).'

As luck would have it, a young rocker, twenty years or so younger than the women, was walking past. For some reason, the word 'mosha' caught his attention. With a stupid grin on his face, he butted in, 'Hey, my sisi, did you say we're moshing?'

To this, our distraught entrepreneur lashed out uncharacteristically (she was hurting): 'I am not your damn sisi, laaitie. But, yeah, you're moshing. You're moshing everything. Everywhere.'

Without missing a beat, our young rocker skipped off, screaming, 'Whooo! Mosh. We're moshing.'

He was obviously on drugs – as were our two entrepreneurs, by the end of the night.

The rest is history.

Anyway, can we all just stop uku (to) mosha. Tu,[42] because everywhere you look, people are at it.

If you see a friend chatting up a married woman, tell him, 'Uya (you are) mosha.'

---

42 'Tu' is a colloquial term for 'please'. I am not sure how this came to be. I suspect we naively thought that, when Afrikaners said 'toe', they meant 'please'. 'Gaan tronk toe' confused us at the beginning. We were like, 'Is this guy seriously asking me to go to jail? WTF? No, thanks. I'd rather not.' But the beatings set us straight and we eventually got the point. By the time they said, 'Gaan Meadowlands toe,' we knew very well that the Group Areas Act was not some polite request. It was too late to drop 'tu' as 'please' though.

If your girlfriend wants to drive drunk, tell her, 'Uya mosha.'

If your preacher husband wants to buy you a car with church money, tell him, 'Uya mosha.'

If your colleague wants to downplay the pain that being called a monkey causes black people, tell her, 'Uya mosha.'

If your business partner wants to capture the state, tell him, 'Uyamosha.' But the state must also stop being so easy to capture. Fok.

Isn't it amazing how often some musicians ruin their own songs? The featured artists will be doing just fine, and the instrumentals will be doing things to you. Then, the main man comes in and ruins everything. Sit down. Uyamosha.

Moshile is when you've caused the damage.

If you've impregnated a woman that is not your wife, umoshile (you've mosha-ed).

If you're in police custody, chances are umoshile.

If people using the loo after you gag, umoshile.

If you're a president who's allowed your friends to capture the state, umoshile.

Kumoshakele is 'it's all fucked'. As in Eskom.

Ungamoshi means don't ruin, damage, or compromise. Every morning before you leave your house, look at yourself in the mirror and say, 'Hey, wena, ungamoshi today.'

ASIXOLISENI

This word is specifically for my Zulu brothers and sisters: asixoliseni – let us ask for forgiveness.

Asixoliseni for state capture. Sure, we didn't invent it and others have been capturing since day 1, but shoo, our people are so implicated in this Zupta mess. Asixoliseni and promise to do better.

Asixoliseni for xenophobia. Again, we aren't the only culprits, but boy, did we go in enthusiastically. How embarrassing.

Asixoliseni for taxi drivers. Yes, not all taxi drivers are abe-Zulu, but you know very well why we have to apologise. Asixoliseni.

Asixoliseni for Zodwa Wabantu. Or not.

Asixoliseni for political violence. Ask for forgiveness and ensure that it never happens again.

Asoxiliseni for 2017's cannibalism. What the actual fuck? Who does that? (I've seen some delicious-looking infants, though.)

Asixoliseni for Life Esidimeni. Qedani is one of ours, right?

Come on, let's show the rest of South Africa the way and apologise for any transgressions in which we're implicated. Other groups have their own problems they need to apologise for, so let's get the ball rolling and hope they'll follow suit.

Asixoliseni.

Select Fan Comments from Facebook

Karin Taljaard: There is Zulu in my head and I love it.

Ann Donnelly: I've lived in Africa for over sixty years and am only now learning about the ashy thing . . . who knew? (See 'Mpunga', p. 184)

> **Melusi's Everyday Zulu:** I'm also learning a lot about white people. Like the isikhokho conversation [isikhokho – the hardened crust of pap or mealie rice that sticks to the bottom of a pot, see p. 41]

> **Sefepi Lejafela Morw Lekgau:** White [people] eat isikhokho, too? Hau banna. I thought vroeg they eat bacon, eggs, omelette, etc. But definitely not isikhokho. Don't get me wrong, I'm just amazed. Enetlek we are the same people, yes we are.

> **Gugu Sithole:** I also would never have thought white people eat isikhokho. These posts are the future, so light-hearted yet so educational.

> **Bronwen Bartlett:** It's because it's so delicious and crunchy . . . nomnomnom.

> **Gugu Sithole:** I know right, enjoy it myself, nom nom nom.

Bronwen Bartlett: Ja, but also if there's leftover potjie or stew and you eat that for breakfast using the crusty pap like a spoon. All cold.

Sefepi Lejafela Morw Lekgau: Lol . . . Wow, this just changed my perception of life. These are the things I considered 'black', if I may.

Judy Koning Pretorius: Melusi, I have began to look . . . to really look in the mirror and acknowledge things like my white privilege. I have begun to, instead of moaning, do a positive thing. I volunteer at a learning centre to help children in an impoverished area to read/speak English. It is not easy to acknowledge some stuff in your life but necessary for personal growth. And I will always repeat this – we need to start loving one another in SA, love must be our morality.

Francois Rousseau: It's like those 'Dear white people' Twitter posts – we don't have a WhatsApp group either. Or, 'you murdered my ancestors' – no, white people isn't an immortal collective like The Borg.

Zwelakhe Zee Tshabangu: We are The Borg. Resistance is futile. Lol!! FellowStarTrekFan

After the word konje (loosely translated as 'by the way') was posted on Melusi's Everyday Zulu:

Buhle Moyo: In Ndebele, we say kanje.

Melusi's Everyday Zulu: In isiZulu kanje means 'like this'.

Buhle Moyo: Interesting. There are quite a few words like this where if you're talking to a Zulu/Xhosa person they look confused. Like when I first moved to the Cape, I was confused when Xhosa people said 'baleka'. For us that means to run away.

Ríona Judge McCormack: Melusi is utterly brilliant – weaving language, politics and vivid imagery in a way that is both hilarious and thought-provoking. Everyone interested in this country should follow.

Frieda Tweehuysen: I love these posts! And I have my colleagues in stitches every day, trying out the words.

Eike Köhler: Love Melusi's posts – I am trying to learn Zulu here in Germany. Maybe one day soon I can come to South Africa and practise my pronunciation!

Tracy Clifford Statt: Ouch . . . oh man, looking back at those pass laws and that brutal apartheid bullshit is so painfully embarrassing. But I choose to read this with thanks for bringing me into your world of experience and enlightening me to the way expressions entrench themselves long after the event. Correct my rusty school Zulu if needs be . . . Ngiyabonga.

Anita de Bruyn: Greatest thing that could have happened to bring all South Africans together so we can start to really understand each other and work together for a better future for everybody!

Endnotes

I. Ngibonga means I thank (I = ngi, thank = bonga).
Ngiyabonga means I am thankful or I am thanking (someone).
Ngiyabonga also means thank you.

II. Phaphist is not an isiZulu word. It is my anglicised version of phapha.

III. Lilizelas is not an isiZulu word. It is my anglicised version of lilizela.

IV. Khumbuza-ed is not an isiZulu word. It is my anglicised version of khumbuza.

V. Fakaza-ing is not an isiZulu word. It is my anglicised version of fakaza.

VI. Sala-ed is not an isiZulu word. It is my anglicised version of sala.

VII. Chama-ed is not an isiZulu word. It is my anglicised version of chama.

VIII. Ndaba also means news.

IX. Shelaring is not an isiZulu word. It is my anglicised version of shela.

X. Bekezeling is not an isiZulu word. It is my anglicised version of bekezela.

XI. Vova-ing is not an isiZulu word. It is my anglicised version of vova.

Acknowledgements

▼▲▼

First and foremost, I'd like to thank Mark Zuckerberg. The Facebook founder takes a lot of flak, but Facebook has been good to me, so Mark has me in his corner.

My mother co-wrote this book, because she instilled the love of ubuZulu in me. I doubt she'll be happy about being associated with some of the colourful language it contains, though.

Then, my wife and kids, my source of inspiration in everything I do.

Of course, I also thank fellow abeZulu for existing. But not all of them. Some are just terrible people.

Last but not least, I thank all my social media followers. If it weren't for them, I doubt the publishers would have given me a second thought.

About the Author

▼▲▼

MELUSI TSHABALALA is a seasoned creative professional and entrepreneur with a career in advertising spanning twenty years.

He is co-founder and managing partner at Studio 214, a Johannesburg-based advertising and design agency. His agency's ethos is to 'create work that touches Africans, inspiring harmony, prosperity and the celebration of this electric continent, her people and their phenomenal cultures'. Melusi strives to uphold this ethos in his everyday life too.

His greatest joy comes from the laughter of his three wonderful children, for whom he hopes to help build a better African future.

Since Melusi started with his Everyday Zulu Facebook posts in October 2017, Everyday Zulu has been a regular feature in *Finweek* and on Saturdays with Jenny (Crwys-Williams) on Kaya FM. He also has a slot on East Coast Radio's Breakfast with Darren Maule and has been featured on Ukhozi FM.